Mission-Rich *AND* Profit-Powered

ISBN: 979-8-9895715-0-5
ISBN E-Book: 979-8-9895715-1-2

Cover Design: Justin W. Hardin of Damascus Media

Photography:
Jon Jones of J81 Studios LLC
Darrius Mylze Johnson of Visionary Acts

Editors:
Miriam Arvinger of The Writing Expert
Patricia Hill (Work Mom)

For more information visit:
www.missionrichandprofitpowered.com
www.monroenaylor.com

Table of Contents

Dedication

This book is dedicated to you who are in my strong circle. Over the years I have been blessed to have church leaders, mentors, and friends who have inspired and encouraged me to set and accomplish goals. I value your time, love, and wisdom.

I also dedicate this book to my family. I am especially grateful for my husband Mah'dee Naylor, Sr. and mother who have been my biggest supporters. I also must acknowledge my children (Naomi, Patience, Mah'dee Jr., and Melodie), my dad, siblings, and sister friends.

Last, but not least I dedicate this book to the loving memory of my Nana, Joyce Marie Vaughn. My heart cries for you daily and I am so thankful for the work ethic and integrity that you ingrained in me through your unwavering love.

Introduction: Mission-Rich *AND* Profit-Powered

This book is for those who believe that each day can be better than the last, who understand the value of giving to receive, and who trust that God provides for their journey. I, too, share this mindset, which made it challenging to follow conventional routes to business success. My commitment to authenticity and integrity is rooted in my faith, which has inspired my search of God's grace and promises, as stated in Jeremiah 29:11.

Money, it's often the foremost concern for most business operators, whether in the for-profit or non-profit sector. But for those driven by a mission, grounded in faith, their purpose takes precedence. These mission-rich individuals, often called social entrepreneurs, navigate a less profitable path with a smile, driven by compassion and a deep desire to improve the lives of those around them.

In the business world, there's an unspoken code suggesting that to profit, one must work the longest hours and sometimes betray others behind their backs. This code differs from my beliefs and what I teach my children. Yes, I've attended business school, graduate school, and various programs to bolster my credentials. These programs provided valuable insights, but they don't fully explain my success in raising millions of dollars for my business and co-founding a non-profit with just $500, which is now on track for a $1 million budget in less than five years.

My faith has been a cornerstone, as have my supportive family, friends, and mentors. I've never forgotten my humble beginnings, the obstacles I've overcome, or the drive that led me here. Beyond the biographies and online content, I'm a woman who grew up amidst adversity, witnessing crime and violence regularly. I remember the apartment complexes and co-op housing where I lived, a place where prostitution, drug dealing, and violence were unfortunately commonplace. Despite this environment, I drew inspiration from my father's military travels, which exposed me to a broader world. I also had a remarkable community of angels around me who saw beyond my angry face, bad attitude, and quick temper. They recognized my tenacity, passion, and intelligence.

One traumatic event, however, stands out amidst the chaos of my upbringing. It was on December 23, 1996, while walking home from a music studio, that my life took a harrowing turn. Robbers attacked my friend, and in the ensuing struggle, a gun went off. A .38 caliber bullet struck me in the chest. To say it changed my life is an understatement. It was the most pivotal moment of my entire existence.

That pivotal event, though life-altering, is not what this book is about. It's about the words I uttered when I believed I was breathing my last, "Lord, I am not fit to live, and I am not fit to die." Those words, spoken in the shadow of a near-death experience, continue to resonate with me. I saw the light, but it was not a divine light. It was the ambulance, and the next time I saw a light, it was the face of my preaching grandmother, waiting as the ambulance let me out. She said, "The

Lord had me praying for you for the entire noonday prayer hour. He spared your life, so what are you going to do about it?"

There were many lessons learned over the nearly 30 years since that night. I've used those lessons, combined with my business acumen, to develop what I consider to be a recipe to guide mission-rich individuals off the road less profitable. In the following nine chapters, you'll discover how to bring your full self to your mission while creating a strategy for a fully funded, profit-attracting business.

You don't need to compromise your identity to succeed; you can be Mission-Rich *AND* Profit-Powered. As Deuteronomy 28:13 states, you are the head, not the tail, and lead without sacrificing your values. And as my preaching grandmother once told me after that life-altering moment, "He spared your life, so what are you going to do about it?"

CHAPTER ONE

Mindset

I believe there is a call to mission-rich ventures. I also know there are a lot of myths. I call it the myth of Charity versus Non-profit and Social Entrepreneur versus Profitable Mission-Rich LLC. In the world of mission-rich businesses, there are certain myths and truths that I had to unlearn along my journey. These revelations have been instrumental in my understanding of what it truly means to operate a mission-rich business.

Dispelling Optics of Mission-Rich Non-Profit and For-Profit Businesses

Mission-Rich Non-profits

Non-profits are expected to be mission-based according to the definition in the 501c3 tax code. At the beginning of my entrepreneurial journey, I often found myself entangled in the optics of charity versus running a nonprofit business, which led to conflict amongst leadership within the organizations. It's essential to distinguish between the two, even though both are driven by a sense of purpose and making a positive impact. A charity is often seen as an organization that provides services or resources without the expectation of a financial return. In contrast, a nonprofit business operates with a clear mission, and an understanding that generating profits is crucial to sustaining its operations and expanding its impact. Understanding this distinction allowed me to recognize that making a profit is not a sign of selfishness but a necessity to continue doing good in the world.

Mission-Rich LLCs

There are also myths and misconceptions that often surround mission-rich LLCs. Many mission-rich entrepreneurs who start LLCs tend to undercharge or give away their services as if they forget that their business was created to make money. However, similarly to non-profit entities, the truth is that a mission-rich LLC should balance profit and purpose. Your business can generate revenue while staying true to its mission and values.

I am dispelling the myth that a mission-rich entity must prioritize purpose over profit. Your business can and should aim for both. It's time to break free from these limiting beliefs and create a business that ensures financial sustainability while making a positive impact. Remember, your business was created to make money, and there's no shame in that if your mission and values remain at its core.

My Start

My journey started with a yearning that felt like it had been simmering for an eternity, though I can recall it like it was yesterday. I was caught in a relentless cycle of seeking guidance and information from various people, desperately trying to find the missing pieces that would enable me to launch a non-profit when I was appointed by my pastor to work on a grant writing project. We spent hours and hours completing grants and submitting them only to find out that we were not eligible. We had no idea what we were doing. I would reach out to consultants, lawyers, nonprofit leaders, and church leaders – but to no avail. People would say, "Oh I can show you how we did it." I am still waiting for some of them to call me back.

I felt taken advantage of as I spent hundreds of dollars on programs, grant certification programs, and workshops to learn what to do. What I found out was that no one really knew what they were doing. The memory is vivid. I was frustrated and felt like I was trying to fit a circle into a square because I had a vision of what it was supposed to be, but no one understood what I was trying to do.

One day after praying about the situation, I went to Google and typed in some phrases that led me to the nonprofit management program at a local college. I knew nothing about the program, but I was determined to meet the deadline to enroll, which was one week away. I diligently got all the work done to apply and submitted it. When I graduated from the program, I vowed that I would do whatever I could to be equipped to help individuals who have passion work, whether a ministry, general non-profit, or for-profit entity, and empower them to transform it into a funded business. Since that day, I resolved to embark on this path filled with determination but lacking the knowledge and access to funding.

Here I am on the threshold of something that has been simmering for nearly six years, now bursting forth into reality. This is the moment where I finally heed the call of my higher power to share the gifts that have been placed within me—the gifts of administration and helping others. My mission is simple: to empower individuals to take their mission-rich ideas and transform them into businesses, whether they be for-profit or non-profit. I want businesses to not only survive but thrive. I want them to experience financial growth while allowing their creators to focus on what matters most—your families.

The COVID-19 pandemic was a harsh teacher. It taught us that life is precious and that our pursuits should be about more than chasing a quick dollar. We realized that despite the relentless emphasis on the American dream and the virtue of hard work, our families were the very heartbeats that fueled our endeavors. We woke up early and labored late into the night to provide for them, to ensure they had food, clothing, and a safe place to call home.

But we also recognized the limitations of the old way of doing things. Many of us discovered that our zeal was there, but our knowledge was lacking. We didn't know how to start and sustain a business, let alone one with a mission at its core. The statistics speak volumes. I have watched countless entrepreneurs end up closing their businesses, and the same with non-profit organizations is no different. Countless non-profits are launched each day, but most struggle to pay their staff, let alone cover their expenses and maintain a comfortable lifestyle.

Mission-rich individuals aren't seeking to amass vast wealth from their non-profit organizations. However, too often they find themselves caught in a whirlwind, driven by the desire to help others to the point where they treat their business as a charity.

In the chapters that follow, we will explore the keys to success in creating mission-rich and profit-powered ventures. I won't perpetuate the myth that hard work guarantees prosperity. Hard work alone is not a sustainable or rewarding path, and it won't lead to a happy marriage, successful children, or a life free of regrets.

Let's journey together as we navigate the framework to turning your mission-rich dreams into profitable realities, all while keeping your loved ones at the forefront of your purpose.

Unlearning Myths and Discovering Truths about Mission-Based Business

My journey into the world of mission-based business began with countless misconceptions and assumptions. People often assume that running a non-profit or a mission-focused for-profit business means you can't make money. There's also the myth that a great idea for helping people, animals, or a noble cause is enough to secure funding. Some believe that being a non-profit means have to scrape pennies to operate, and people should just understand that.

The reality is that starting and running a business involves more than meets the eye. It goes beyond the bureaucratic red tape and government regulations, digging into what I call the ABCDs of mission-driven and profit-driven ventures – crucial elements I wish I had grasped when launching my enterprises. While many focus on the technical aspects of business initiation and management, I firmly believe and have experienced that mental resilience is fortified through a holistic approach that combines faith and a harmo-nious work-life balance.

Moreover, this unwavering determination distinguishes genuine entrepreneurs and business leaders from what I refer to as "wannapreneurs" and "amipreneurs."

-   Wannapreneurs: These individuals sell services or products haphazardly, lacking structure and a well-thought-out plan.

- Amiapreneurs: They sell services, often for a third party, and receive 1099-MISC or 1099-NEC forms at the end of the tax year, running inconspicuous businesses.

The ABCDs encompass unique aspects that aren't typically taught in traditional educational settings. They are highly personal and can be challenging to explain in a classroom. Nonetheless, I am determined to help you understand their importance in the journey of starting a business. The 'A' in ABCD stands for "Activatable Passion," and this is where I began my journey.

"A" Activatable Passion Unmasked

Here, I want to share a personal story that relates to discovering your activatable passion. Before starting my most recent businesses, I recall being on a mission to start a daycare. Someone I held in high regard had suggested it to me because I had several children, and they thought it would be an easy transition. I listened to this advice multiple times and even took steps to get certified and start the daycare. However, a mentor posed some tough questions that made me realize it wasn't my true passion. It wasn't my activatable passion because I did not want to spend my day changing diapers or speaking to toddlers all day. I loved doing it as a mom, but at some point, I needed and wanted a break from little people. The lesson here was to never pursue something solely based on others' advice or expectations. Your strong "why" should be the foundation of your activatable passion, something that you deeply believe in and can sustain over time.

Activatable passion goes beyond fleeting or situational passions—those momentary sparks of enthusiasm that arise in specific circumstances. Temporary passions are just that—temporary, often fading as the initial excitement wears off. For instance, you might become passionately involved in advocating for your child's needs at school when faced with a challenge, only to realize later that you lack the long-term commitment to advocacy.

Situational passions, on the other hand, are born from the context you find yourself in. For example, when my family experienced temporary displacement due to a flood, I felt passionate about real estate investment, inspired by the profits hotels were making. However, when we returned home and the situation changed, so did my enthusiasm for the venture.

But true activatable passion is the kind that keeps me awake at night, occupying my thoughts even when I'm exhausted. It provides me with the strength and energy to persist in my efforts day after day because I love it that much. It's the driving force behind my every action.

In my own life, this passion became evident when I realized the importance of advocating for my son in a school environment. Although his sisters did really well in a local charter school, he struggled in the second grade. My son was getting written up and suspended requiring us to miss work often to check-in on him. It got to the point where he was recommended to see a therapist although we knew there was nothing he needed a therapist for. The school accepted no accountability for what my son was experiencing, they called him "defiant" and "disrespectful." But, when their therapist recommended medication as a response to my son's outbursts, we sought another solution. The short of it is that a friend working for the local district shared that the local elementary school had improved. We found this to be true and transferred our son to his zone school. Within weeks, we were called by his teacher who shared that an incident had occurred. The teacher started the conversation by sharing how smart our son was. It was the first time we heard any compliments about him in a year, but I inquired about the incident. The teacher shared what occurred but stated it wasn't what he did that alarmed her but why he did it. She shared that our son had been traumatized. After crying, I gathered myself when she said, "I want to help you help your son." From that point I worked with the school advocating for my son and other students.

My activatable passion wasn't just about advocating for my children; it was about helping people learn what they needed to achieve their goals and missions. It extended beyond K-12 education to equipping individuals to launch and run businesses, whether nonprofit or for-profit, in line with their passions.

I discovered that my true calling was to empower people, and my journey led me to create a nonprofit organization and become a business consultant. As you continue reading this book, you'll learn how I managed to balance work, family, and faith while building my businesses. And you'll see how my activatable passion became the driving force behind all my endeavors, ultimately leading me to celebrate a 20-plus-year marriage and the successful journeys of my children into adulthood.

"B" - Banking your time - Charging for My Services

An early struggle in my consulting journey was understanding the value of my time and services. I used to undersell my expertise, believing that people couldn't afford it. I even offered free workshops to attract clients. However, I learned the hard way when someone who attended my free sessions considered my $25 webinar as too expensive. This revelation made me realize the importance of valuing my time and identifying my target audience. I stopped chasing clients who didn't appreciate the value I provided and instead focused on enhancing the quality of my services. This shift allowed me to move from charging $25 per hour to $100 per hour in the first year of my consulting business, *(eventually higher than that) as I shifted my focus towards social entrepreneurs and away from "wannapreneurs."*

Bankable time is when you are operating within your passion, and the time you're spending is valuable to someone to the extent that they are willing to pay for it. Bankable time doesn't mean charging people for every minute of your time—it's about providing value through your work, driven by your mission-rich focus.

There's a common notion that we must determine our worth and charge a certain amount for our time, which often makes us stingy with our time. But bankable time isn't solely about charging for your time; it's about providing so much value that people are not just willing but eager to pay for what you offer.

The key is adding value. Bankable time is not about chasing dollars; it's about chasing impact. We must understand that, while we're not solely driven by money, we can't fund our mission without it. As Peter Brinkerhoff, often regarded as the godfather of nonprofit work, wisely said, "No money, no mission."

So, how do we make our time bankable? It's not about just giving away our expertise for free. It's about providing value in such a way that people see the worth in what we offer and are willing to invest in our mission. I learned this through my journey.

When I started my consultant business, I had a wealth of knowledge that I was eager to share with others. I provided free workshops and gifted complimentary consultations to about 45 people. What I found was that while many appreciated the information, only a small number saw the value in my time and were willing to pay for it.

I realized that people often don't value things that are given for free. So, I began to charge a modest fee, gradually increasing it as I saw more people appreciating the value I offered. The structure of my proposals, and the reasonable amounts I charged, played a crucial role in making people more willing to pay me for my services.

Value isn't just about the information you provide; it's also about how you deliver the information and ensure that it serves a purpose. Bankable time is about providing value that resonates with your target audience, and that's what turns your time into something people are willing to invest in.

Understanding who your ideal client is, conducting market analysis, surveys, focus groups, and offering samples or complimentary sessions are essential in identifying those individuals who truly value what you bring to the table. These are the people who become not just clients, but also ambassadors for your work, always speaking well of you and supporting your mission.

Bankable time is about adding value in a way that resonates with your audience and turning your time into something people are more than happy to pay for. It's a balancing act that can propel your mission forward while ensuring that it's financially sustainable.

"C" - Capacity to Balance Work and Life."

Balancing work and life can be a significant challenge for entrepreneurs, especially those with a mission-rich mindset. There were times when I felt guilty about pursuing more and going beyond the expectations set by my culture or community. People with scarcity mindsets might project their fears onto you, making you feel guilty for wanting more in life. However, it's essential to be strategic and intentional about how you use your time. I started identifying time-wasting activities and redirecting that time to grow my business. I also prioritized self-care, family, and relationships by strategically scheduling them into my calendar. It's about creating a harmonious balance that allows you to thrive in both your personal and professional life.

Balancing work and life is not something that happens by chance; it's a trained, intentional, and strategic process. Many people mistakenly believe that running a profitable and mission-rich business means managing a multimillion-dollar entity while their marriage falls apart, and their children run wild. Let me emphasize this: being mission-rich is not about building wealth at the expense of your family's well-being. Mission-rich work is about legacy, where "everything (or one) attached to you wins", as gospel recording artist Jekalyn Carr beautifully puts it. However, they won't win if you can't find that balance and bring your family along with you on this journey.

In the upcoming chapters, I'll discuss strategies you can implement to ensure you don't work alone. I'll address how you can strengthen your relationship with your spouse while nurturing your business, and how to intentionally allocate time and create periods of commitment to prioritize both your business growth and your family. I'll explore how to set up family meetings, family time, and even incorporate business meetings into family trips. The goal is to make everyone feel that you are all in this together and growing together, even if it's at your own paces. This is incredibly important because without it, you might end up being miserable.

I've always made it a priority to center my life around Christ, with my family coming right after Him. I've made sacrifices throughout my career to ensure I was present for my family as much as possible. My husband and I balanced our work schedules and child-rearing responsibilities. My mother played a crucial role in providing a support system for our children. She was someone who was close to them, paid attention to them, loved them, and cared for them. This will look different for every family, but the point is that we need to find what works for us, for our spouses, and for our children.

How do you ensure you're not bringing the stresses of your work life into your home environment and turning it toxic? How do you make sure that your work doesn't become your spouse, and your projects don't become your children? These are critical questions that need intentional and strategic answers because if you don't make it a priority, work will take over and prioritize you. You'll receive phone calls about your child's behavior at school, notice the cold shoulder from your spouse, and maybe even hear rumors of infidelity or disconnection. No one wants that.

We want to preserve the love and commitment we have to our partners and family by adding to it rather than letting it erode. In the same way that we are to be strategic about business, we must be strategic and intentional because we are not just business owners – we are business leaders. You have to show people that it's possible to simultaneously focus on both your professional and personal worlds. And both worlds can work together seamlessly. You are not going to get it 100 percent right every time, and there will be challenges, but people must see you setting the example as the leader and forerunner of your enterprise. They need to see that it is possible to balance your work and your personal life because both matter. This is how your passion will shine through your work and show that you have taken care of what's most important to you, and that passion will radiate in everything you do.

"D" - Delivering with Excellence and Empathy

In my journey as a mission-rich entrepreneur, delivering excellence and empathy have been non-negotiable aspects. When I co-founded a non-profit, we emphasized providing high-quality services from the very beginning, but we didn't stop there. We recognized that excellence goes hand in hand with empathy. Excellence ensures that our programs and services are of the highest quality, while empathy allows us to understand the needs and feelings of those we serve. This combination creates a profound impact. When our marketing agency experienced the quality of our programming and our empathetic approach, they were eager to help us reach our true audience with respect, compassion, and top-notch quality. Empathy isn't just about what you do; it's about how you make people feel.

In mission-rich businesses or non-profit organizations, there's sometimes confusion between mission-driven work and charity. Many mistakenly believe that making a profit isn't essential, but even in the nonprofit sector, generating income is critical to fulfilling the mission. Moreover, delivering services and products with exceptional customer service should never be overlooked.

For instance, I co-founded a non-profit organization around five years ago, and we're now heading into our sixth year. When we embarked on this journey, our financial resources were quite limited – just about $500 from my bank account, co-signed by my supportive husband. As we gradually secured a few grants here and there, we've always adhered to a commitment to excellence.

We asked ourselves, how can we provide services like meetings, brainstorming sessions, focus groups, or youth events in a way that people would perceive as being professional, led by individuals who genuinely care about the work they're doing? This commitment to excellence remained steadfast, whether we were operating with a modest budget of $50,000 or the half-million-dollar budget we recently managed. As we move towards reaching that million-dollar milestone, our commitment will continue.

Excellence isn't about just meeting expectations – it's about going above and beyond. I clearly remember how we initially named our services "victim services" since we primarily assisted people who had experienced various forms of trauma, including domestic violence, bullying, and harassment. But a pivotal moment came when one of our clients expressed her discomfort with being labeled as a victim. She told us she was a survivor, and we listened.

We immediately made the change to "survivor services" to respect her perspective and that of others who might feel similarly. Our commitment to excellence extends to every aspect of our work. It involves being responsive to feedback, remaining flexible, and acknowledging that we don't have all the answers. It also means taking a good look at the words people use to describe us and our services. We've asked our board, clients, and long-term supporters to share their perceptions through word clouds. If the words used don't align with our intentions, we know it's time to focus on empathy and excellence.

"D" also represents "deliver with empathy." We strive to make sure every interaction with our business or non-profit leaves people feeling valued, heard, and cared for. We are all in the people business, first. People want to work with YOU when you deliver with empathy. They will pay whatever price, donate to your cause, and contract with YOU first because they like you.

Here are some strategies I've personally found invaluable. I understand that embarking on a journey to achieve something new requires a shift in mindset. If I could already do it with my current mindset, I would have succeeded by now. That's why I've embraced the need for change and growth. And you may need to do the same.

Significant external events often trigger a cataclysmic shift in mindset. In my case, the challenges of the COVID-19 pandemic, the loss of people I knew and loved, and an inner knowing that it was time to grow, were the driving forces behind my shift. To achieve my vision, I committed to professional development, training, leadership classes, and invested in my growth. I had to accept that nothing changes without a shift and I had to be ready to embrace it.

At the core of my mission-rich business is the deeply ingrained value of empathy. This empathetic approach forms the bedrock of everything we do, allowing us to authentically connect with the people we serve, be it our valued clients, our dedicated team members, or the communities we engage with. It's the emotional intelligence that keeps us attuned to their needs, aspirations, and struggles, helping us tailor our services for the maximum benefit of all involved.

This enduring commitment to empathy is born from my personal journey, a path paved with trials and tribulations that instilled a profound sense of compassion and understanding. I experienced so much stress that it led to anxiety attacks (camouflaged as asthma attacks because my doctor did not know the difference. My parents separated when I was about seven years old causing life as I knew it to spiral into unrecognizable circumstances. I had been violated by a trusted adult, shot and almost killed by a relative who attempted to rob my friend, and grew up in a home where vices were commonplace. To say I was angry is an understatement. I was also emotionally a nd spiritually wounded and full of insurmountable levels of complex trauma.

In spite of the trauma that I experienced, I still found a way to push beyond those circumstances. Day-to-day struggles had become my norm, but I distinctly remember my teenage years, around 16 or 17. I learned to take city buses to journey to nearby towns, determined to grasp the intricacies of applying for college scholarships – my ticket to higher education because my financial resources were nonexistent. I was never one to back down from challenges. I did things like enroll in honors and AP classes, participate in extra-curricular activities, and volunteer in student government. I was fully committed to forging a brighter path for myself than I had seen in neighborhoods of my community.

One pivotal moment etched in my memory because of an individual's empathetic leadership was a school suspension I faced after an in-school physical altercation. In the face of judgment, I summoned the strength to advocate for myself. However, my advocacy was not required because my school counselor, Mr. Singleton, allowed his hilarious yet compassionate perspective to identify an alternative solution for me. He decided to exclude the altercation from my school record, safeguarding my scholarships for my college aspirations.

During all this, I sought solace in youth programs and turned to the art of writing poetry and crafting music as coping mechanisms. These creative outlets played a pivotal role in preserving my emotional well-being and helping me navigate the tumultuous waters of my youth as a Black girl.

These experiences and feats of life throughout my childhood into adulthood strengthened me to grapple with the challenges I faced later in the corporate and public sector and church worlds. Despite witnessing the often impersonal nature of business transactions, these experiences have fueled my passion to create an enterprise that breaks these stereotypes. My story is that of many who strive, recognizing that behind every project or partnership, there are real people with dreams, hopes, and sometimes daunting obstacles.

In the realm of entrepreneurship, empathy isn't just a feel-good concept; it's a dynamic force that propels meaningful change. It's the catalyst behind our constant drive for innovation and the engine that powers our commitment to helping others navigate their unique paths to success. This strategic and heartfelt approach transcends traditional business norms, fostering sustainable growth and amplifying the transformative impact we aim to achieve in our mission-rich endeavors. It's about more than just business; it's about fostering a genuine connection and leaving a positive, lasting mark on the world.

Discover Your Activatable Passion

As you navigate the world of mission-rich businesses, remember that unlearning myths and discovering truths is an essential part of the process. What's most important is discovering your activatable passion and understanding your strong 'why.' To guide you through this journey, I recommend creating an ABCD worksheet. This worksheet will help you align your mission, goals, and strategies while also ensuring you maintain a strong sense of purpose and profitability in your mission-rich business.

Call to Action: Ignite Your Mission-Rich Journey

As you've unpacked the myths, truths, and personal anecdotes within this chapter, it's time to ignite your mission-rich journey. Here's how to take the first steps:

1. Reflect on your strong "Why": Take a moment to introspect and define your strong "why." What motivates you? What's the deeper purpose behind your business endeavors? Your strong "why" will be the driving force behind your activatable passion.

2. Evaluate Your Value: Just like the shift I made in my consulting journey, assess the true value you offer. Don't undersell yourself. Recognize your worth and charge accordingly. Attract the right clients who value your expertise.

3. Prioritize Excellence and Empathy: Strive for excellence in everything you do but remember that empathy is the heart of impact. Understand your audience's needs and feelings. Let empathy guide your actions.

4. Balance Work and Life: Learn to balance your mission-rich business with your personal life. Don't feel guilty about wanting more or pursuing self-care. Prioritize your well-being and relationships alongside your entrepreneurial aspirations.

5. Take Action: Create a strategic plan to align your mission, goals, and strategies. Use the ABCD worksheet as a guide to ensure that your mission-rich business remains both purposeful and profitable.

Your mission-rich journey is about creating lasting impact while achieving your personal and professional goals. Take these steps today, and let your passion and purpose propel you toward success. The world needs more mission-rich entrepreneurs like you.

CHAPTER TWO

Complexes and Sabotage

Unpacking Mindsets and Complexes

There are several complexes that have held me back when it came to launching and leading a profitable mission-driven business. I share these because I have also observed these same complexes hinder my colleagues and clients.

We will explore the various types of self-sabotage that we often engage in due to ingrained mindsets and behaviors that limit our potential. We will dive deeper into these mindsets, which can hinder mission-rich business owners and social entrepreneurs. These mindsets include the martyr complex, the quest for shortcuts found on YouTube, entitlement, being broke, cheapness, and procrastination.

The Martyr Syndrome has been a significant hurdle for me, and overcoming it has been a journey of self-discovery and growth. The persistent belief that I must constantly sacrifice myself, even to the point of detriment, has impacted various aspects of my life. There were times when I prioritized helping others over crucial moments with my children, missed much-needed vacations, and even dismissed date nights with my husband—all in the name of fulfilling what others said they needed, but really only wanted.

I came to the realization that people will allow you to do as much for them as you choose to. It was a tough lesson. I found myself setting aside my dreams to enable others to pursue theirs, leading to my unwelcome companionship of jealousy, bitterness, and depression in my heart.

At my core, I am not a jealous or spiteful person. Discovering my faith allowed me to adopt a mindset of empathy and perspective. I could even empathize with the person who shot me because I saw the hurt and trauma that led them down that path. However, as I overextended myself for years in the name of being a Christian, I began to feel bitter and depressed. It was like running on a hamster wheel, expending energy but going nowhere.

A turning point came when I desperately needed love and concern from those I had always been available for. I realized, after they made no effort to show up for me, that they didn't have to do anything for me. So, I questioned myself about feeling that I needed to do everything for them. The answer, I am not God. I cannot answer all things, be all things, or be everywhere. That realization became the starting point for my journey towards breaking free from the Martyr Syndrome.

Rejecting the Martyr Syndrome wasn't just about preserving my mental and spiritual stability—it was about saying "yes" to my family, my husband, my loved ones, and, most importantly, to myself. Above all, it was about saying "yes" to God first. I had lost sight of the true purpose of my service in my relentless giving. That's when I resolved to shift my focus from comparing myself to others and their accomplishments to working diligently towards my own goals.

There was no room for bitterness if I was filled with purpose and being a good steward of the gifts and talents that I was blessed with.

To navigate this transformation, I employed the ABCDs to develop a personal strategic plan and identified those I could rely on for support. Saying "no" to the Martyr Syndrome became a powerful step toward reclaiming control over my life and aligning my actions with my authentic self. I was able to see beyond the limitations of my eyes and the individuals I thought my life was indebted to. I found the strength to be of "good courage" and be assertive because I understood that I would not and could not please everyone. Although I knew that when Martyr Syndrome held me captivated, I was in denial, but I know the truth and now I am free.

Martyr Complex: This mindset revolves around the belief that success requires sacrificing every waking hour. You may feel that you're not doing enough if you're not exhausted, falling asleep at your desk, or barely able to rest. However, such a mindset can lead to burnout and negatively impact your business and well-being.

Addressing the Martyr Complex:

The martyr complex can lead to burnout and physical or emotional health issues. Recognizing the need for balance in your life is essential. Seek guidance and support to overcome this complex and understand that saying "no" when necessary is not a sign of weakness but rather a path to sustainable success.

Quick Fix YouTube Syndrome: Some individuals seek shortcuts to success, relying on YouTube gurus who promise quick riches without effort. They overlook the value of hard work and learning from experience, hoping for immediate results.

Beware of Quick Fixes:

Be cautious of seeking shortcuts to success through YouTube influencers. Ensure that those you follow, and trust are genuinely experts in their field. Keep in mind that true success often requires dedication, effort, and learning from both successes and failures.

Entitlement: Entitled individuals believe that others owe them something because they started a business. They often reject advice and assume they already know everything. This mindset can hinder personal and professional growth.

Combatting Entitlement:

Avoid falling into the entitlement trap. Understand that you should choose partners, clients, and team members based on their value and the benefits they bring to your business. Don't be afraid to charge what you're worth and recognize that others should do the same.

The Broke and Cheap Complex: Even when one has the resources, this mindset involves behaving as if you don't. It may prevent you from investing in your business or leveraging available resources. Focusing solely on the bottom line can limit your business's potential.

Like the broke complex, being excessively cheap involves seeking the lowest-cost options in every situation. This approach may hinder your ability to maximize resources and investments.

Overcoming the Broke and Cheap Complexes:

Don't limit yourself by behaving as if you're broke or constantly seeking the cheapest options. Investing in your business and resources can often lead to more significant returns in the long run. Consider the value and return on your investment rather than just the cost.

Procrastination: Procrastination manifests differently in each individual. It can derail progress and productivity, whether it's due to personal avoidance or external distractions. In recent years, I have heard various experts link procrastination to mental and emotional imbalance caused by stress, trauma, or health.

Tackling Procrastination:

Recognize the forms of procrastination that hinder your progress, whether they are self-inflicted or caused by external factors. Create a plan to allocate your time more efficiently and stay committed to your goals.

The Everlasting Battlefield of Mindsets:

One of the most challenging aspects of overcoming these complexes is unlearning deeply ingrained beliefs. It's essential to distinguish facts from personal truths that may have been shaped by your upbringing, experiences, or social environment. God's truth, as found in His word, can liberate you from these limiting mindsets and guide you toward personal and business growth.

Some of the most used items in my toolkit for my continuous improvement have been self-reflection, identification, and action. Through these, I have learned to own that I am the leader of my organization and business.

- Self-Reflection: As the leader of your business, it's your responsibility to identify and combat these complexes. Implement a continuous improvement plan, encompassing both personal and business growth, guided by your spiritual connection. Seek opportunities to reflect on your journey and assess your mindset to ensure that it aligns with your mission.

23

- Identification of Weights: Identify the weights that hinder your progress, whether they're personal, spiritual, or business-related. These may include unresolved issues, financial challenges, or the need to develop new skills. Once you've recognized these weights, create a plan of action to address and overcome them. Oftentimes, the focus is on the things that other people are doing to you, but how are you responding to these obstacles? This is where taking the time to identify what is hindering you is integral to the ability to shift your mindset and capability to sustain – regardless of the challenges or why they exist.

- Action: Learn from Positive and Negative Experiences: After enduring your experiences, both positive and negative, we must be intentional and learn valuable lessons throughout the process. Don't only focus on what not to do but also embrace the positive aspects and behaviors that can lead you to success.

Once I started recognizing these self-sabotaging behaviors, I had to figure out what to do about it. Did I need to sign up for a training course? Go on a business trip? Take a vacation? Maybe just have a day at the spa? I needed to find a way to redirect myself so that I wouldn't keep falling into that same old slump. If you want to move your passion work along and establish a profitable business, you must develop your customized system to exposing and getting rid of self-sabotaging behaviors. Know that you will have days when you do well and others when you do not stick to your plan. But, if you reset every day, you can get rid of debilitating behaviors and attitudes that hinder your ability to grow and be the business leader that you are capable of.

Identifying the triggers and the people around me who were enabling these behaviors was crucial. I realized that I learned the most from observing the faults of others, especially in terms of what not to do. It's easy to say, "I would never do that," but what about the things I should do? I needed to be intentional about learning those as well.

Conclusion: When I Knew I Had to Do Better

The complexes that tend to hold back mission-rich individuals often stem from behaviors learned in our youth or young adulthood. They're behaviors that hinder us from becoming the leaders we aspire to be. I remember hitting a breaking point where I was on the verge of a nervous breakdown. I was 7 months pregnant with my fourth child, with three children under five, and my husband was experiencing health scares. On top of that he was self-employed, I was working full-time, and we were extremely active in our church. I was empty from exhaustion. Still, I kept giving of myself to the point where I was literally shaking in my car trying to text my supervisor to take a day off from the employee lot. I somehow made it to church and found myself crying at the altar for hours.

At the end of my four-hour crying session, I heard a voice asking me, "If something happens to you, who will take care of your babies?" I looked up and realized no other person was in the sanctuary but me. That was a turning point for me. I knew I had to let go of relationships that had been suffocating me, and the idea that I had to say "yes" to everything just because I'm a Christian woman. I decided to seek guidance and ended up in a one year sabbatical before enrolling in a leadership institute.

I was randomly selected, though I believe it was a divine appointment, to work one-on-one with a coach from the leadership institute. The coach, who happened to be a borderline atheist, challenged me to pray to my God for guidance, as he could see how unhealthy my tendency to overcommitment had become. I took up that challenge, prayed for guidance according to my faith, and opened my Bible. It was like a sign from above when I read, "Let your communication be yea or nay, whatsoever is more than these comes of evil" (Matthew 5:37). It was a profound moment of release. I realized I could say "no."

But, a few years later, I found myself right back in the same situation. My calendar was filling up with commitments that didn't make sense, and again I was running empty, which was affecting my health. I was gaining weight and experiencing health issues like fibromyalgia symptoms and migraines. I decided it was time to act and prioritize my well-being.

I sought alternative health solutions, went through a 90-day detox, and prayed for my mental and emotional wellness. During my prayer, I had a revelation that I needed to cut the "fat" out of my life, both literally in terms of losing weight and figuratively by removing anything that didn't align with my core mission and values. Identifying and acknowledging your mindsets and complexes will help you determine what you need to bring out the best leader in you. It could be recognizing the need for self-care, setting boundaries, or aligning your actions with your true purpose.

Call to Action:

Identify which of these complexes resonate with you and acknowledge their impact on your business and personal growth. Develop a plan to counter these mindsets and create a systemic approach to continuous improvement. Take the necessary steps to ensure that your mindsets align with your mission and purpose.

CHAPTER THREE

Breaking Free from the Comfort Zone

The comfort zone is a dangerous place, emphasized by a former colleague, who used to encourage me to join her in yoga classes. Her words weren't just about stretching the body; they were a call to stretch the boundaries of what's familiar and comfortable. Those words have stayed with me, making me reflect on what activates that inner passion that compels us to step outside our comfort zones.

My journey into entrepreneurship didn't happen overnight. It was a culmination of experiences that slowly eroded my contentment with the corporate world. It all began with a constant feeling of being undervalued at my job, despite my relentless efforts and long hours.

I found myself on the verge of career advancements many times, only to be told that my experience fell short. Rejections were like thorns in my side, but instead of letting them deter me, they fueled my ambition. The first time I had the confidence to apply for an executive level job, I came in second and was told that I didn't have enough experience. The second time I finished in second place I was told the same thing. I figured it was me and I needed to improve my skillset and credentials. I decided to gain the expertise I needed to make a real difference. It was a period of humility and growth when I decided to seek validation, not from my superiors, but through skill development.

Not long after my second position rejection, I came in second a third time. At that point, I began doubting myself and barely tried the fourth time. I then decided that if my jobs could give me executive level tasks to complete then I had the ability. I finally saw the glass ceiling that I heard so much about and decided that I would bust through it. But, it would not happen in the way I was conditioned to believe. My breakthrough would come through the spirit of entrepreneurship that I ran from for many years, but finally realized that all of those doors were shut so that I could open this one.

If I told you I woke up excited about being a business owner and that things fell into place immediately, I would be lying. Despite my dedication, I remained the perennial runner-up for key positions. Rejections stung, but it also propelled me to pursue opportunities where I could volunteer my skills and gain practical experience. I offered my time without expecting anything in return, knowing that practical experience was worth more than gold. Which is what I found out when I ran for School Committee in my city. I was a candidate with no political ties or formal training, but I ran a skillful campaign and won the first time which is a rare feat.

This period was a crucible for my personal and professional development. I learned to navigate corporate politics, build resilience, and humbly accept that I couldn't control the biases of decision-makers. As I honed my skills in my volunteer work, I encountered another crucial aspect of growth — humility. Acknowledging my limitations and areas for improvement was painful, but integral to my transformation.

Turning Point of Acceptance

The turning point came when I embraced the harsh reality: my job wasn't the path to fulfilling my true potential. It wasn't an easy acknowledgment. I had invested years of energy and effort in my corporate career, and it was painful to admit that my vision for my future differed from the organization's.

The final blow was when I sought new job opportunities. Despite commendations and contributions to major projects, I was repeatedly told I lacked the experience. My self-esteem took a severe hit, and I started doubting whether I'd ever make the progress I aspired to achieve.

The pressure only grew as I dealt with personal hardships and losses, including the death of loved ones. The fragility and unpredictability of life hit me hard, intensifying the urgency of pursuing my mission. I knew that if I didn't take the leap and follow my passion, I'd forever wonder "What if."

During these struggles, I had a pivotal experience during my leadership academy. One of the challenges was to spend a night outdoors, making s'mores with my peers. The thought of venturing into the woods, surrounded by darkness, triggered memories of my fear of the unknown and my discomfort with unfamiliar environments. But I remembered that I had embarked on this leadership journey to push my boundaries, challenge my fears, and grow as a person and a leader.

Despite my reservations, I decided to step out of my comfort zone and join my fellow participants at the campfire. As I toasted marshmallows, laughed with my peers, and shared stories under the starlit sky, I realized the significance of embracing discomfort. This experience

29

wasn't just about s'mores; it was a symbol of my determination to overcome my fears and barriers. It was a testament to my commitment to personal growth.

Use Your Muscles – Confidence and Resilience

These experiences, both personal and professional, led me to the moment where I decided to embark on the entrepreneurial journey and start my consulting business. It wasn't a decision I took lightly, but it was fueled by a burning desire to no longer settle for a career that didn't align with my ambitions, my skills, or my mission to help others achieve their dreams. Starting my own venture wasn't merely a career move; it was a declaration of faith, a testament to the belief that I could make a more significant impact by aligning my passions and skills. It was my confidence embodied in action.

The obstacles I'd faced were no longer deterrents; they were the catalysts that drove me to venture into the unknown. Through these struggles, I found my strength, my purpose, and my determination. The support and love of my family and the faith that sustained me guided my journey to becoming an entrepreneur. The adversity and hardships I faced led me to this pivotal moment, and I embarked on my entrepreneurial adventure with a commitment to excellence, empathy, and a passion to create a profound and lasting impact in the world of mission-rich business consulting. These were the pillars of my resilience; they reminded me of "whose" I was and what His plan was for me.

The Devil We Know

Our comfort zones are a double-edged sword. They encompass the things we're comfortable with, whether they are normal or dysfunctional, traumatic or healthy, toxic or beneficial. We tend to use our comfort zones as a shield against fear. When faced with the unfamiliar, the challenging, or the uncharted, we retreat to what's safe, to what we're used to – the familiar, the okay, the comfortable.

The irony is that what we're comfortable with might not be what's best for us or our families. It also is not always normal or functional. Yet we do what we know because of what may happen if we try something that we have never done or that no one we know has ever done.

I can relate to this from personal experience. I once lived in a neighborhood that had become increasingly dangerous over the years. It was rife with gang violence, shootings, and instability. But I stayed there because it was what I was used to, having grown up in similarly tough environments. I, myself, had been a victim of gun violence, but it was the norm that I had grown accustomed to.

Despite desperately wanting to move to a safer place where I did not have bullets flying through the walls of my house, fear held me captive. What could be more fearful than knowing whether one of your children might be struck by a stray bullet in the middle of the night? The fear of the unknown, the fear of change, the fear of leaving behind the environment I had become accustomed to. This fear was like a straitjacket, preventing me from pursuing a better life. But it was what I knew, what I was "comfortable" with. I had a clear bias against anything and anyone I was unfamiliar with and, in my mind, it was okay.

We like what we know and who we know. I cannot tell you the number of times that I chose to work with someone on the sole basis of knowing them. When I say this, I am not necessarily talking about people who you would identify as toxic or bad people. I discuss toxic relationships later in this book. Right now, I am talking about folks you would call like-minded. Everyone wants to be in the company of like-minded people because they don't challenge the equilibrium. I have had to learn to seek after like-hearted people because I do not improve my thinking, systems, or anything if everyone thinks just like me and sees the world just like me. But, if they have similar fundamental values as me, that will create a level of synergy that become contagious.

Like-hearted people challenge you to think differently and see things differently.

Conclusion: Remember Your Strong Why!

This is why we need to be cautious about our comfort zones. These fears can paralyze us and affect every facet of our lives, including our careers, families, and relationships, as we try to push beyond the familiar into uncharted territory. And then there's that ever-present shadow – imposter syndrome. It's the feeling that you don't deserve the success you've worked so hard for, even though you're more than capable. The nagging thoughts of the fear of failure or the fear of success can imprison you.

Before you contemplate starting a business, you need to focus on your strong "why." You must constantly remind yourself of the driving force behind your actions. This might mean telling yourself two or three times a day, adding affirmations, scriptures, or declarations to keep your motivation alive, or even enlisting the support of loved ones to remind you during moments of doubt. It likely means adding some individuals to your circle or network that are different from your usual suspects. It likely means going to a networking event alone, traveling to a conference alone, or hiring a vendor that you never would have worked with before but are now willing to try.

Your strong "why" will be your anchor in the storm, your guiding star, always keeping you focused and motivated. Sometimes, you might need to approach it from different angles, but you must remain excited about it because it's your guiding light. The more you focus on it, the better equipped you'll be to overcome the obstacles that will inevitably come your way, trying to keep you in the same old place.

One key strategy is to examine your life and recall moments when you decided to embark on something new and then stopped. These moments can help you identify what repeatedly emerges when you approach the brink of your comfort zone. Another element of this is to do something like 20 Answers where you give yourself space to come up with more than one response or solution to an issue. The primary question to ask yourself is, "What would someone who wants to start a _____ business do to grow it?" After you make your list, try something from that list at least once every week, and do not allow yourself to back down from the challenge. You will not die! It will be okay! You are building your muscles of confidence and resiliency.

Referring back to the story of me at the bonfire. It was one of our challenges to spend the night at a camp in the middle of no where. My fear of the unknown and the woods held me back. But I reminded myself that I set out to push my boundaries and, after a couple of hours warring with internal struggle, I joined the group outside. Overcoming this fear was a powerful experience, and it became a growth moment in my quest to push beyond my comfort zone.

The same fear that had gripped me in childhood, stemming from my experiences in a tough neighborhood, had followed me into adulthood. These fears can translate into our professional lives, making us hesitate to seek donations, share our business plans, or even believe that we deserve success. We carry these fears with us, and they become stumbling blocks on the path to achieving our goals.

Call To Action

Embrace the Unknown and Expand Your Horizons - To take the next step, conduct a passionate assessment to understand what truly motivates you. Create a personal systemic approach, a plan to stretch beyond your comfort zone. Understand that activating your passion, reminding yourself of your "why," and breaking free from your comfort zone are crucial steps toward creating a mission-rich, profitable business. It's not just about what you do – it's about who you become in the process, as you step into the unknown and grow beyond your comfort zone.

1. Reflect on Your Strong "Why": Take some time to reflect on your core motivation, your strong "why" – the driving force behind your aspirations and endeavors. Write it down and make it tangible. This "why" will be your guiding star on your journey to push beyond your comfort zone.

2. Engage in a Passionate Assessment: Conduct a passionate assessment of your life and career. What truly motivates you? What ignites that inner fire? Identify the source of your passion and make it a focal point of your actions.

3. Create a Personal Systemic Approach: Develop a strategic plan to push beyond your comfort zone systematically. Consider your comfort zone as an elastic band that needs stretching. Define the areas or experiences where you've hesitated in the past and devise actionable steps to confront those fears.

4. Seek Encouragement and Support: Don't go on this journey alone. Share your "why" and your mission with trusted friends, family, or mentors. Enlist their support in times of doubt and ask them to remind you of your motivation when you need it the most.

5. Step Outside Your Comfort Zone: Identify opportunities to step outside your comfort zone in various aspects of your life. Remember the s'mores experience in the woods during my leadership academy? Leap, even if it feels uncomfortable at first. These small victories will empower you to take bigger steps.

6. Combat Imposter Syndrome: Recognize the signs of imposter syndrome and confront it head-on. Remember that your journey is grounded in your passion and experience. Embrace the belief that you are deserving of the success you seek.

7. Seek to Align Your Passion with Your Work: In your professional life, seek opportunities to align your passion with your career. If you're considering entrepreneurship, think about how you can translate your mission and passion into a profitable business. You can create a profound impact.

8. Practice Self-Compassion: Be kind to yourself as you navigate uncharted territory beyond your comfort zone. Acknowledge your efforts and celebrate your achievements, no matter how small. Self-compassion will keep you motivated and resilient.

9. Document Your Progress: Keep a journal of your journey. Document your experiences, challenges, and successes. Reviewing your progress can provide motivation during moments of self-doubt and inspire others who are on a similar path.

10. Inspire and Mentor Others: As you grow and expand beyond your comfort zone, share your story with others. Mentor those who are looking to do the same. Be the guiding light for someone who needs that extra push.

Remember, your mission-rich journey isn't just about what you do; it's about who you become along the way. You have the strength, the passion, and the inner drive to create a lasting impact and achieve your goals. Break free from the confines of your comfort zone and step into the unknown with confidence. The world is waiting for your unique contribution.

CHAPTER FOUR

Lead with Authenticity and Empathy

One of the aspects that truly resonates with me when I reflect on the journey of turning a beloved passion project into a fully funded business is the profound significance of empathy. It's a facet often overshadowed in discussions about running a mission-driven business, mainly because many individuals tend to overlook the far-reaching impact it has on those in our orbit. What's more, the effort required to embrace this level of humility can seem daunting, especially when it contradicts the prevailing notion that as one ascends, one's importance increases. However, it is precisely those who aspire to make the greatest impact who must be willing to take a backseat to allow grace into the front seat, to foster lasting, meaningful change. This facet is something I hold close to my heart, and it's intricately woven into the tapestry of my journey, from leaving my job to embarking on my consulting business venture and leading the growth and expansion of a nonprofit organization.

Empathy is not just a nice-to-have quality in the realm of mission-rich business; it's indispensable. I often liken empathy to the heartbeat of my venture, the foundation upon which I built my business. It's the capacity to genuinely understand, connect with, and care for the people I serve, from clients to team members to partners.

Emotional Intelligence (EQ) is something that has become more of a trending topic over the last 5-7 years. In 2017, the Harvard Business Review identified: Self-Awareness, Self-Management, Social Awareness, and Relationship Management as the key facets of emotional intelligence, with empathy lying within the Social Awareness category. However, recently experts have added empathy as a separate category due to the unique set of challenges it takes to reach a healthy level of empathy that positively impacts a business and organizational culture.

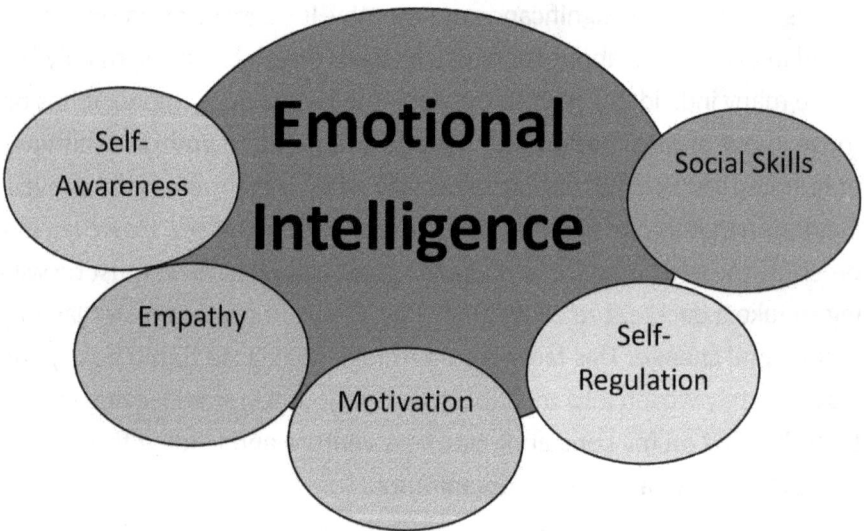

The reason I place such a significant emphasis on empathy is that it's an acknowledgment of the humanity in each of us. It's the recognition that every individual has their unique challenges, fears, and aspirations. For those I work with, empathy signifies that I not only hear their concerns but truly understand them on a deeper level. It's about being there with an open heart and an open mind, ready to support, uplift, and guide them, often beyond the confines of the business itself.

Types of Empathy

There are three primary types of empathy.

- Cognitive (thinking/logic): Ability to see another person's perspective. This is often observed as under-emotional as it has more to do with the mind and logic. This can lead to assessing a situation without emotion although the perspective is visible.

- Emotional (heart/feeling): Ability to feel someone's pain and emotion. This is often observed as being over-emotional and can lead to burnout and taking on the baggage of others, which is unhealthy.

- Compassionate (action/doing) - relating to someone's pain and moving forward to assist and is the recommended display of empathy. This is the balance of the other two forms of empathy and is the most authentic.

When talking about empathetic leadership, I am talking about compassionate empathy. It is the healthy type of empathy that goes beyond merely shouldering someone else's emotions or burdens. Cognitive empathy feels distant to people because if you have not "walked in someone's shoes" you really can't demonstrate the authentic experience. Emotional empathy, which is something I am very familiar with, can result in the pitfalls of compassion fatigue and vicarious trauma and is a common challenge faced by individuals in ministry and mission-based enterprises. This is the type of empathy that often leads to nervous meltdowns in mission-rich individuals. The objective, therefore, is to cultivate a form of empathy that is both compassionate and balanced. However, this endeavor requires a sophisticated skill set that many people tend to use sporadically.

For instance, when caring for a loved one or nurturing a child, empathy often comes naturally. In these roles, we find the capacity to forgive and forget their past mistakes, to recognize their untapped potential, and to actively collaborate with them to help realize that potential. We devise various strategies to support and empower them along the way. Whether it's because we derive personal satisfaction from their success, which enhances our image as parents, or because we genuinely yearn for their triumph. This form of empathy often flows generously.

Surprisingly, when we transition to our roles in businesses or ministries, we often establish demanding expectations for our staff without extending the same guardrails, varied communication styles, or the willingness to invest in their growth that we readily provide for our loved ones. Yet, it's these very individuals who play a pivotal role in the success and prestige of our businesses and missions.

Empathy's Role in Business

In the context of running a mission-rich business, empathy begins with the people you aim to serve. For instance, let's consider clients seeking my consulting services. It's crucial for me to genuinely comprehend their challenges, goals, and the emotional and practical hurdles they may be facing. This isn't just about providing a service; it's about addressing their deepest needs and desires. The empathetic approach doesn't merely stop at delivering the necessary solutions but ensures that the clients feel heard, valued, and cared for throughout the process.

Within a Team

Empathy is equally vital in my relationship with my team members. It means understanding their strengths and weaknesses, aspirations, and struggles. It means acknowledging the effort they put in and the personal sacrifices they make for the success of the business. It's about creating an environment in which they feel not only professionally appreciated but also emotionally supported. In turn, this leads to a highly motivated, cohesive team that genuinely believes in the mission we're pursuing.

It also ensures that they won't leave you without recourse, but instead will leave their position better than how they found it and more likely assist you with finding a good replacement. Better yet, they have probably already trained someone internally to take over their role.

Within Collaboration

Partnerships and collaborations are another arena where empathy plays a pivotal role. It's about recognizing the unique strengths and objectives of the organizations or individuals we partner with. This approach allows us to tailor our collaborations for maximum impact, forging alliances that go beyond the transactional and toward shared visions.

How empathy shows up in partnerships and collaborations is through recognizing the unique strengths and objectives of our partners. Being empathetic to their needs allowed us to create alliances that are not merely transactional but built on shared visions. The ability to see beyond the immediate business goals and genuinely connect with our partners has led to more meaningful and productive collaborations.

Within Constituents

Empathy doesn't end with the immediate stakeholders. It extends to the beneficiaries of our mission-rich work. By understanding their needs, challenges, and aspirations, we can fine-tune our services and offerings to create a more meaningful and lasting impact.

To implement this form of empathy, when I develop strategic plans, I make it a point to truly understand my clients. I don't just offer solutions; I want to be a compassionate partner on their journey. The stories of clients facing complex challenges and seeking my support taught me that genuine empathy can turn a business transaction into a deeply rewarding personal experience. It's the understanding and care they receive that fosters long-lasting relationships, resulting in clients who feel heard, valued, and confident in our partnership and share the positive sentiment with others. One of my coaches often says, "You treat someone right and they will tell six people. You treat someone bad, and they tell 3000."

When operating at our highest level of empathy we can shift our societal impact on the local and larger landscape. This lens equips us to be aware of broader challenges and disparities. In my experience, this awareness has always led to a shift in strategy and a more effective approach to my work. It has demonstrated that empathy is not static; it's a driving force that compels us to adapt, change, and improve. It's about contributing to social change and community empowerment, making our mission-rich business not just about profit but about creating a positive impact on the world. When we do this right, people pay attention and will look for ways to partner with you and patronize your business.

Empathy Realized

Empathy also means listening, and sometimes, it means adapting. There have been instances where I've started with one idea or strategy, only to realize that it doesn't fully align with the needs of my clients or the community I serve. It was through empathetic listening that I was willing to pivot and evolve. The ability to say, "I hear you, and I'm here to support you differently" has been a game-changer.

Of course, empathy isn't just about what's said or heard; it's about the feelings that resonate during every interaction. It's about the warmth that underlines the client call, the compassion in the guidance, and the understanding in the partnership. This has been manifested through strong relationships and long-term clients who value not just the services but the care they receive along the way.

Furthermore, empathy extends beyond the business realm into the community and society we serve. It means being aware of the broader challenges and disparities, and considering how we can contribute to social change and community empowerment. My consulting business doesn't merely aim to improve individual organizations but also seeks to uplift the communities these organizations serve.

Empathy Prevailed

In the context of struggles that led me to entrepreneurship, empathy was a beacon of light. It was born out of my own experiences of feeling undervalued, unheard, and at times, overwhelmed. I knew firsthand the pain of yearning for support and understanding and decided that my business would stand as a symbol of hope, compassion, and transformation for others. This is what I wanted people to feel when they encounter any of the businesses or projects that I oversee.

Empathy is the cornerstone of the client relationships that my business is built upon. A Catalyst survey of 900 individuals confirmed that empathy is the driving force that positively impacts employee retention, innovation, inclusivity, and work/life balance. (Van Bommel, T. (2021). It's the secret ingredient that makes my services not only professional but deeply personal. It's the reason clients don't just receive assistance, but feel that they have a partner in their journey toward success.

In the world of mission-rich business, empathy isn't a passive sentiment; it's an active force that drives change, fosters growth, and elevates the impact of every endeavor. It's what allows me to deliver with excellence, making every engagement a testament to the passion, care, and deep understanding of the people and communities I'm privileged to serve. This is where authenticity enters. To be true to our empathetic self, we must be authentic with ourselves to understand where we truly lie on the spectrum of empathy.

Path to Empathy - Authenticity

Late at night, when no one else is around, play back your day to see if you showed empathy. If you did, when and why? If you did not, when and why? The essence of our ability to show empathy comes from being true about who we are and honest about what we have done. Yes, you may do things out of bad habit, hurt, bitterness, or trauma – but own it! Be honest because the only path to freedom is truth.

My research and lived experiences have taught me that empathy is a transformative force. I've walked the path of feeling undervalued and overwhelmed, and it was the empathy of those who supported me during those times that made a significant difference. Whether it was my high school counselor Mr. Singleton, life mentor Mrs. Dora

Robinson, or my Nana whose understanding and willingness to listen with their hearts alleviated my struggles and inspired me to pay it forward. I realized that my business should embody that very same empathy, becoming a guiding light for others facing challenges. It's in the strength of my personal struggles that I discovered the profound impact empathy can have, making it a cornerstone of my business philosophy.

Never did the empathetic ear that was lent to me approve of my misconduct, bad attitude, or fault. But it made me feel heard and valued. It made me realize that I am more and could be more than I was displaying at that moment. The occurrences of being attacked by mental and emotional setbacks are part of life and will follow us into business.

In essence, my life and successes are a testament to the transformative power of empathy. They have shown me that empathy isn't just a soft skill; it's the very heartbeat of my mission-rich business. It's what makes my business a source of hope, compassion, and transformation for clients, team members, partners, and the broader community. It's a force that drives change, fosters growth, and elevates the impact of every endeavor I pursue.

However, I have not always embraced empathetic leadership, because it required me to dig into places that I had covered and issues that I had buried so deeply that I would sometimes forget. One day, I looked at all my mentors and realized the primary characteristic they had in common was their empathetic leadership coupled with a level of unmatched authenticity and humility. It was then, that I became determined to focus on personal development and training in areas like trauma-informed care, DEIB (diversity, equity, inclusion, and belonging), cultural humility, effective communication, time management, facilitation, and leadership.

I must highlight some of the personal development training that has enabled me to establish an empathetic identity in leadership:

- Trauma-Informed Care: Personal development through trauma-informed care training is a powerful pathway to empathetic leadership. Understanding the impact of trauma on individuals allows leaders to approach their team members, clients, and partners with greater sensitivity. The stories of clients who may have experienced trauma emphasize the need to create a safe and supportive environment. It's through trauma-informed care training that I've learned to approach individuals with empathy, recognizing that their past experiences may influence their present. This training equips leaders to provide not just solutions but compassionate support, fostering trust and resilience within their teams and clients.

- Diversity, Equity, Inclusion, and Belonging (DEIB) Training: DEIB training is instrumental in promoting authentic leadership. This chapter highlights the importance of connecting with individuals from varying backgrounds and social statuses. DEIB training offers insights into different perspectives and cultural nuances, providing leaders with the tools to communicate and lead authentically across diverse settings. The stories of forging partnerships with organizations from various cultural backgrounds underscore how DEIB training can be a bridge to building genuine connections. Leaders who prioritize diversity, equity, inclusion, and belonging create a culture of respect and understanding, where every voice is heard and valued.

- Effective Communication Skills: Effective communication is at the core of both empathy and authenticity. There is a great benefit in exploring and becoming proficient in diverse communication styles. I have success stories of pivoting strategies based on client feedback highlighting how versatile communication is an effective two-way process. Personal development in effective communication equips leaders with the ability to listen actively and respond thoughtfully. It ensures that messages are conveyed with clarity and empathy, promoting trust and openness in the workplace. My story of personal growth and evolution demonstrates that leaders who hone their communication skills can build stronger connections and inspire their teams and clients effectively.

I incorporated these elements into this chapter to reinforce how personal development and training are pivotal in the journey toward empathetic and authentic leadership. They provide the tools and knowledge necessary to understand and connect with others on a deeper level. By actively investing in these areas, leaders not only enhance their own growth but also create environments where empathy and authenticity flourish. This, in turn, leads to stronger, more resilient teams and lasting, meaningful impact in mission-rich businesses.

Why People Resist Using Empathetic Leadership

From my observations, I've noticed that people may exhibit resistance to empathy for a range of reasons. It's essential to approach this subject with a deep sense of understanding and compassion, acknowledging that everyone's experiences and viewpoints are indeed one of a kind. It's crucial to grasp how empathy, when wielded without prudence, can sometimes lead to unintended negative consequences. This awareness is key to ensuring that we avoid some of the outcomes that can trigger resistance in people such as:

- Fear of vulnerability: Many individuals fear that being empathetic might expose their vulnerabilities, making them feel exposed or uncomfortable.

- Misperception of empathy as weakness: Some people mistakenly believe that showing empathy is a sign of weakness, when, in reality, it's a demonstration of strength and emotional intelligence.

- Self-focus: In a fast-paced world, we often become preoccupied with our concerns and may not take the time to consider the feelings and experiences of others.

- Cultural and societal norms: In certain cultures, or social environments, empathy may not be strongly encouraged or valued, which can shape individuals' behavior and beliefs.

- Lack of understanding: Sometimes, people may not fully grasp what empathy entails or how to practice it effectively, which can deter them from embracing it.

Do not allow the possibilities of how empathy can go awry to be the reason you do not pursue enhancing this skill. It's important that you observe that empathy is a skill we can cultivate and foster, both within ourselves and others, inspiring them to lead with greater compassion and understanding. In this process, it's worth acknowledging that people may discover their capacity for empathy through the empathy we extend to them, as often, the empathy we receive mirrors the empathy we offer.

How I Have Benefited from Empathetic Leadership

To provide you with a counter to why people resist empathy as a tool of leadership, let me share how I have observed the growth in my capacity and network due to my consistent practice of working through an empathetic lens. Some of the areas I can easily identify are:

- **Consistency in Authenticity:** I believe that one of the corner-stones of authentic leadership is the ability to remain true to oneself in all aspects of life. I've always strived to be the same authentic person, whether I'm in a business meeting, picking up groceries, or attending church. This consistency is not just important; it's a necessity. It shows people that my character and values remain unwavering, regardless of the circumstances.

- **Building Trust:** Trust is something I've always held dear, and authenticity and empathy play a crucial role in building it. When people meet the same authentic me in various situations, they begin to trust not just my words, but my actions as well. They see that I live by my values consistently, and this consistency is what engenders confidence. It's about being the person I claim to be, and this, in my experience, is what builds a strong foundation of trust in both professional and personal relationships.

- **Long-Lasting Relationships:** Authenticity and empathy, as I've come to realize, are instrumental in creating strong and long-lasting relationships. When individuals encounter the same person in different settings, they can relate to me on a personal level. It's not just about transactional business interaction but about connecting with another human being. This personal connection often transcends into lasting relationships based on mutual respect and understanding.

- **Reflecting My Brand:** I've always believed that everything I do contributes to my personal brand. From the way I answer the phone to how I respond to emails, it all reflects my brand, which is an extension of my values and authenticity. When people meet the same person across various situations, it re-inforces the brand I've worked hard to build. My brand reflects who I am, and it's not just about what I say but how I live those values in every facet of my life. This consistency strengthens my personal brand, attracting like-hearted individuals and opportunities.

In my journey, I've found that embodying the same authentic and empathetic leader across all aspects of life is not just a choice; it's a necessity. It's not about compartmentalizing my persona but about living my values consistently. This builds trust, fosters enduring relationships, and reinforces my personal brand. When people meet the same person, regardless of where they encounter me, it's a testament to my unwavering commitment to authenticity and empathy in leadership.

I remember a profound conversation I had with one of the presidents of a foundation that had the pleasure of funding my non-profit. He shared a perspective that has stayed with me throughout my journey. He said, "The true testament of an organization's success is the demonstrated vision and passion of its leader and the ability for the board and staff to align with the leader's vision and passion." This statement resonated deeply with me and reinforced the significance of authentic leadership.

Conclusion: Establishing a Culture of Compassion

This chapter serves as a powerful reminder of the importance of establishing a culture of compassion and respect within an organization. This culture isn't solely the responsibility of leaders, but it's something that should be preferred and championed by everyone involved, from leaders to team members. This culture reflects the values that underpin the organization's mission.

Assessments of communication, personality, decision-making, and conflict resolution are all vital components of nurturing this culture. These assessments are more than just tools; they are the building blocks of an environment in which compassion and respect thrive. They guide us in understanding how to interact with one another, how to honor individual strengths and weaknesses, how to make informed decisions, and how to navigate conflicts with grace and empathy.

Incorporating this insightful perspective into the narrative emphasizes the importance of authentic leadership in creating a culture of compassion and respect. It underlines that this culture is a collective effort, one that involves leaders, team members, and all stakeholders. By prioritizing assessments and actively working on communication, personality dynamics, decision-making, and conflict resolution, we can foster an environment where empathy and authenticity are not just words but lived principles. This is the foundation of a mission-rich business, where everyone is aligned with the leader's vision and passion, creating a powerful force for change and growth.

Call to Action: Empathy Self-Assessment Checklist:

Here's an empathy self-assessment checklist to help you reflect on and improve your empathetic abilities:

Section 1: Self-awareness

1. I take time to reflect on my own emotions, values, and biases.

2. I recognize the impact of my emotions on my interactions with others.

3. I acknowledge my strengths and areas for improvement in practicing empathy.

Section 2: Active Listening

4. I give my full attention to others when they are speaking.

5. I avoid interrupting or immediately offering solutions during conversations.

6. I ask open-ended questions to encourage others to share their thoughts and feelings.

7. I practice patience by allowing others to express themselves fully.

Section 3: Perspective-Taking

8. I make an effort to understand the viewpoints and experiences of others, even if they differ from my own.

9. I can describe the emotions and thoughts of others based on their perspective.

10. I consider the context and background of individuals when interpreting their actions or words.

Section 4: Emotional Support

11. I offer emotional support and comfort to others when they are facing challenges or difficulties.

12. I express empathy through body language, such as maintaining eye contact and using open and inviting gestures.

13. I validate the emotions of others, letting them know that their feelings are understood and accepted.

Section 5: Empathy in Action

14. I take proactive steps to help others when they are in need, whether it's a friend, colleague, or stranger.

15. I adjust my communication style to suit the preferences and comfort level of the person I'm interacting with.

16. I demonstrate empathy not only in my personal life but also in my professional relationships and interactions.

17. I actively seek feedback from others to assess the effectiveness of my empathetic responses.

Section 6: Continuous Improvement

18. I regularly seek opportunities for learning and personal development in areas related to empathy.

19. I am open to feedback from others about how I can improve my empathetic abilities.

20. I set specific goals for enhancing my empathy and track my progress over time.

Use this checklist periodically to evaluate your empathy skills and identify areas where you can further develop your ability to understand and support others. Remember that empathy is a skill that can be honed and improved with practice and self-reflection.

Strong Networks

Chapter Five of "Mission-Rich and Profit-Powered" digs into the intent of building strong circles, a topic that strikes a chord with me on a deeply personal level. It's a reminder of the profound importance of surrounding ourselves with the right people, not only in our professional lives but in our personal journeys as well. This, because I know that I wouldn't have had the success if I have experienced without the shouldering of the like-hearted and talented individuals.

As my brother in the faith often says, "Your network is your net worth." This profound quote underscores the significance of strong circles in our lives. It highlights that the value we derive from our connections, relationships, and collaborations is immeasurable, ultimately defining our success and the contributions we make to the world.

Strong Network:

Our strong network encompasses the various relationships that must be built and maintained to be successful in our businesses. These relationships impact us on so many levels and are designed to maintain a certain level of distance to be effective. We don't bring everyone home to dinner so we should not air our laundry to everyone we meet. Furthermore, we should not burn bridges because those will be the very ones that hinder us from getting to our destiny or cause us to take longer on the journey to a profit-powered business.

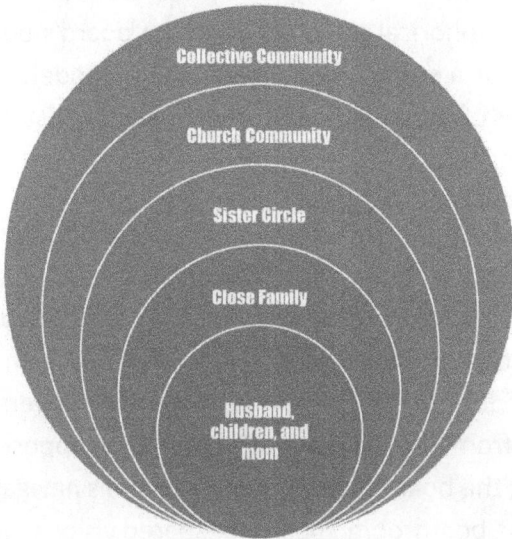

The Significance of a Strong Board:

Just like you, I've experienced the challenges of building a strong board for a nonprofit organization or corporation. (If you have a for-profit business, even if it is an LLC, you have a board, but you are the only person who holds a seat in each of the positions. You would benefit from identifying ad-hoc or honorary "board" members to assist you). It's more than simply a requirement; it's about bringing together a group of individuals who share the passion and vision of the organization. I've learned the hard way that a hastily assembled board with members who don't fully understand or support the mission can be detrimental.

In the intricate dance of boardroom dynamics, I found myself entwined in a narrative where the cherished principles of our 501c3 organization were threatened by divergent visions. Imagine a boardroom transformed into a battleground, where the very essence of our mission was at risk.

I recall vividly likening our struggle to fitting a square peg into a circular hole—a metaphorical clash between the board's pursuit of grants and the need for a sustainable organizational model. In the midst of this, the echoes of our mission seemed to fade amidst the demand for external funding.

Yet, there's more to this narrative—another chapter involving individuals seeking self-promotion. These were individuals who joined my organization with aspirations that extended beyond our collective cause, exploiting our organizational programs for personal gain. Trust was betrayed as confidential information leaked, weaving personal business opportunities from our collective efforts. It was supposed to be about understanding the board members as individuals navigating their own aspirations. The boardroom, meant for shared visions, had unwittingly become a stage for conflicting interests.

These experiences emphasize why your board should align with your mission and its specific needs. A strong board reflects the needs of your organization and ensures you have the skills and capacity to achieve your strategic goals. It's about creating a team that can help you navigate the challenges and seize opportunities as you build and grow your mission-rich organization. It's not about picking your cousins, friends, or random individuals that say they want to be a part of your organization. Your board must be established with intent and strategy.

For instance, picture starting a nonprofit focused on training puppies to be beloved family members. Having someone on your board who isn't an animal lover or lacks knowledge about animal behavior and care wouldn't be beneficial. To build a strong board, it's crucial to have individuals who not only share your passion but also possess the expertise and skills necessary for the mission. This ensures that your board becomes an asset, guiding your organization toward success.

Building a strong board for your nonprofit, as I've discovered, goes beyond the checkbox requirement; it's about gathering a diverse group of individuals who contribute in specific ways:

- Passion and Belief: Board members must share a genuine passion for the organization's mission. Their unwavering belief and commitment to the cause are at the core of their contributions.

- Expertise: Each board member should bring unique skills or knowledge that align with the nonprofit's mission. For example, someone with legal expertise can navigate legal issues, while an animal behaviorist can help understand and address the needs of the animals.

- Connections: The board can leverage its networks for fundraising, partnerships, and outreach. It's their connections that can open doors to resources and opportunities for the organization.

Personal Board of Directors:

My journey has taught me that the people we surround ourselves with profoundly impact our personal growth and well-being. Just like you, I've created my own "starting five." These individuals provide unwavering support and guidance in various aspects of my life. They include friends who excel in areas where I'm looking to grow, mentors who offer invaluable life insights, and experts who provide specialized advice.

These individuals can assist in your personal life, marriage, business, or spiritual walk. In essence, they are people who have been my personal cheerleaders, helping me navigate challenges, make pivotal decisions, and continuously strive to become a better version of myself. They are my trusted advisors in life, not necessarily when it comes to business – though sometimes they help me with that as well. The most important role of these individuals is that they tell me the truth, whether I want to hear it or not. They are not looking for me to love everything they say, but they know that I will respect it because I trust them. Each of them knows how to deliver their guidance as constructive feedback so that it edifies me and builds confidence.

For example, one time I told one of my personal board members that I was struggling with imposter syndrome. He responded that I can't have imposter syndrome because I do the work and know what I am talking about. My problem was that I needed to remind myself of what I knew so that I don't feel like an imposter.

These are the specific characteristics and contributions my "starting five" provide:

- Support and Encouragement: These individuals offer unwavering support, encouraging me in times of doubt and celebrating my successes. Their presence is a source of emotional support.

- Expertise: Whether it's a friend who's a social media guru, a mentor with years of wisdom, or an expert in a particular field, their expertise guides me through challenges and helps me grow.

- Accountability: They hold me accountable for my actions and decisions, pushing me to be the best version of myself. Their constructive criticism keeps me on track.

Mentors:

Mentors have also played a pivotal role in my journey, both personally and professionally. I've learned that while structured mentorship programs have their place, the most profound mentorships often develop organically. It's about identifying those who can guide you based on your unique needs.

For instance, I once struggled with cooking and sought mentorship from individuals in my community who excelled in the kitchen. They graciously shared their expertise, teaching me valuable life skills. When it came to relationships, I sought mentors who had the type of marriage that my husband and I wanted. They would share their wisdom which helped shape our approach to love and covenant as a ministry.

Mentors, in my experience, possess these characteristics and offer these types of contributions:

- Experience: They've walked the path I'm currently treading. Their firsthand experience helps me avoid common pitfalls and make informed decisions.

- Guidance: Mentors provide invaluable advice and share life lessons. Their guidance is tailored to my specific needs, whether it's personal development or career growth.

- Inspiration: Through their achievements and resilience, mentors inspire me to set higher goals and strive for greatness.

Advisors:

When it comes to advisors, I've come to understand the importance of seeking specialized expertise. Just like you, I've been in situations where I needed advice in areas like accounting or legal matters. Choosing the right advisor who understands your unique circumstances can be a game-changer.

I've learned that sometimes, it's worth investing in your business or personal growth by enrolling in programs or seeking advisory services. The knowledge gained from these experts has often proved invaluable in making informed decisions and avoiding costly mistakes.

When it comes to advisors, it's their expertise and contributions that matter:

- Specialized Knowledge: Advisors possess in-depth knowledge in specific areas, such as legal matters or accounting. They provide guidance and solutions to complex issues.

- Strategic Insight: Their ability to see the big picture and offer strategic insights helps me make well-informed decisions that align with my mission or business objectives.

- Problem-Solving: Advisors assist in troubleshooting and finding solutions to complex challenges, ultimately saving time and resources.

Strong Circles:

In my personal and professional life, I've realized that relationships and networks are the cornerstones of success. By surrounding myself with those who share my values and aspirations, I've created a support system that fuels my growth. I've also discovered the power of memberships and organizations that offer valuable resources and opportunities.

However, I've learned to be cautious about who I let into my inner circle. Toxic relationships can drain my energy and hinder my progress. I've come to value my strong circle as a source of healing and rejuvenation, a sanctuary where I can find solace and encouragement. Our strong circles, can have varying characteristics and contributions:

- Positivity and Support: Members of our strong circles offer emotional support, encouragement, and positivity. Their presence helps us stay motivated and overcome obstacles.

- Accountability: They keep us on track by holding us accountable for our actions and decisions. Constructive feedback from these relationships helps us grow.

- Resource Sharing: Strong circles can also contribute by sharing resources, connections, and opportunities that align with our goals.

- Collaboration: Collaboration is a significant contribution from these circles. Working together, we can accomplish more than we would individually.

Strong Team

Now, let's visit another vital aspect of building a strong team which requires something that most mission-rich folks are not good at doing– delegating. However, a word of caution that I have learned and observed. Delegating is a powerful tool, but it can come with risks that go beyond mere monetary concerns. It can affect your image, relationships, and even burn bridges. So, it's essential to tread carefully when it comes to delegation.

Delegating tasks is inviting someone to help with your work. It's a big responsibility that needs careful thought. Oftentimes, I requested assistance without planning what I actually needed. It's like having a guest over without telling them where to go or what to do. We might hear about a job title at a conference and think it fits, but we don't check if it really suits our business.

Nowadays, we have helpful tools like Loom, Otter.Ai, and Zoom. They let us record and explain our daily tasks, making it easier to share responsibilities. We can also use our phones to record how we do things on the computer, like reports or formatting documents. It's not just about giving a job title; it's about making sure everyone understands the role and deliverables to avoid frustration.

Another challenge in the delegation process is picking team members who are not just like us. We tend to choose people who think like we do based on this myth that likeminded people create better working relationships. That's okay when it comes to our expertise, but the tasks we need help with might not be our strong suit.

My experience has been that like-hearted people work better in business because there is diversity of thought, perspective, and expertise. It is vital to your business that you are careful when choosing team members. Do not skip interviews, checking references, or making clear scope of services agreements. Do not hire someone just because you know them or have a personal connection. Delegation is like building a relationship—it needs time and effort. By preparing well, using the right tools, and being mindful of biases, we make delegation more straightforward and effective.

My brother in the faith often emphasizes the direct relationship between our net worth and our network. The circles we form, including our strong circles, influence our positivity or toxicity. If we're not careful about who's in our circle, we may find ourselves miserable, weary, or stressed. Instead of being spaces for healing and rejuvenation, they become sources of stress. The same applies to your team, which can either make or hinder your mission-rich business.

Some strategic tips to consider when building a strong team:

1. Identify Influential Strong Circle Members:

Think about who within your strong circle has a significant influence on your life and mission. These are individuals that you respect and trust. These are also the individuals that you can be the most vulnerable with and who will not judge you.

2. Create a Delegating and Outsourcing System:

Establish a framework for delegating tasks and outsourcing work. This can involve creating videos, flowcharts, and guidelines for different processes. Ensure that the individuals you entrust with work responsibilities know how to meet your level of service delivery. This occurs through training and the ability to communicate your messaging and organizational culture.

3. Change Your Perspective:

Sometimes, we see accounting, for example, as an expense rather than a cost of doing business. Shifting your perspective can lead to smart decisions like delegating tasks. I, for instance, moved away from doing my taxes to hiring an accountant because I realized it was costing me more time and energy.

4. Delegation vs. Outsourcing:

Understand the difference between delegation and outsourcing. Delegation often requires training the person who will take on the task, while outsourcing involves hiring someone proficient in their field who doesn't need extensive training. However, you'll still need to teach them about your branding and how you deliver services or products.

Remember, the people you delegate tasks to, the individuals you surround yourself with, and your strong circle can have a profound impact on your life and mission-rich business. Approach these decisions with care and consideration, and you'll find yourself better equipped to thrive with authenticity and integrity. Your net worth truly is in alignment with your network, and the right team can make all the difference.

The Journey

The success of our mission-driven journeys and business endeavors is deeply intertwined with the relationships we cultivate. These relationships, characterized by shared passion and the specific contributions of everyone, can uplift us, guide us, and propel us toward our goals. It's through these connections and circles that we find the strength and support needed to navigate the challenges and seize the opportunities that come our way.

In the journey of mission-rich and profit-powered endeavors, I've realized that authenticity and integrity are non-negotiable. It's essential to stay true to myself and my values, even as I seek growth and success.

As you embark on your mission-driven path, remember that your network, your team, and your relationships play a pivotal role. Be intentional in your choices and invest in yourself and your mission. With the right support system and a commitment to authenticity, you can make a meaningful impact and achieve your goals.

The Importance of a Proficient Consultant or Coach on Your Team:

Starting a legitimate and legal business is a complex and multi-faceted endeavor. Here's why having a proficient consultant or coach is invaluable as this is the individual/team that supports you as the leader of the business. Everyone in your business comes to you expecting to receive guidance, leadership, or mentorship. As you continue to pour out, you need someone to pour into you.

The blessing of a good consultant or coach for me includes:

- Expert Guidance: I benefit from their proficiency and real-world knowledge in business formation, legal compliance, and strategic planning. They offer tailored insights based on my unique needs and situation.

- Customized Advice: My consultant adapts their guidance to match my specific business structure and goals, whether it's a nonprofit, LLC, sole proprietorship, or an S-Corporation, ensuring I take the right path for my venture.

- Legal Compliance: With their expertise in legal and tax matters, they help me navigate the complex and ever-changing landscape of business regulations and tax laws, ensuring I meet all state and federal requirements to prevent legal issues.

- Streamlined Processes: They simplify the often-cumbersome administrative tasks, paperwork, and filings associated with starting a business, saving me time and ensuring accuracy.

- Risk Mitigation: My consultant identifies potential legal, financial, and operational risks and collaborates with me to develop strategies to manage or avoid them.

- Financial Management: They assist in setting up accounting systems, creating budgets, and developing financial plans to ensure my business's financial health.

- Mentorship and Support: In addition to guidance, they act as a mentor and a source of support, helping me build confidence in my business decisions and overcome challenges.

- Long-Term Success: They help me plan for long-term success, including strategies for growth, fundraising, expansion, and mission fulfillment.

- Credibility and Trust: Having a knowledgeable consultant on my team adds credibility and trustworthiness to my business, which is especially important for nonprofit organizations seeking donations and support.

- Peace of Mind: Knowing that I have a professional guiding me through the process of starting and running my business provides peace of mind. I can focus on my mission and business objectives, knowing that the legal and administrative aspects are in capable hands.

In summary, working with a proficient consultant or coach is an investment in your business's future. It ensures that you start your venture on a solid legal foundation, remain in compliance with the law, and have the tools and knowledge needed for long-term success. The right consultant can make the complex process of starting a legitimate and legal business much more manageable, helping you to focus on your mission and goals.

Trust Your Gut:

I know that I have said a number of times that you must challenge your comfort zone and that you must not be okay with working with people that only think and do things like you. Still, trust your instincts. If you do not feel good about someone, do your research, Google them. Do not allow a bad feeling to settle because someone told you someone is "good". At the same token do not treat someone unfairly because you know someone who had a negative encounter with that person.

There is a difference between challenging yourself to sit in spaces where you are feeling uncomfortable and your discernment kicking in. I have never had a bad feeling about someone go unchecked and anything good come out of it. When we like someone, we ignore the red flags. We are mission-rich people and therefore helpers and inspirers so we believe we can change the person or that they would not do us wrong because of whatever ego we feed ourselves to believe that we are above being slandered or stolen from.

Throughout this book, I have emphasized the importance of stretching beyond your comfort zones and embracing diverse perspectives. However, I want to gently encourage you to honor your instincts and navigate these spaces with a compassionate discernment.

If you find yourself uneasy about someone, don't hesitate to do your research! A simple act like a Google search can unveil valuable insights. Resist the urge to let discomfort linger, especially if you only opt to work with them or allow them in your space because others label the person or company as "good." It's crucial not to base your feelings solely on second-hand information.

Conclusion: Taking the Step to Build Strong Circles

I recognize that there's a delicate balance between pushing boundaries for personal growth and recognizing when your instincts are guiding you. I've found that dismissing uneasy feelings about someone seldom leads to positive outcomes. It's essential to acknowledge the difference between challenging discomfort for growth and discerning when your inner wisdom is signaling caution.

You must give yourself guidelines to follow. For example, I learned that I have a motherly way about me and it causes me to give people many more chances to mess up what I have worked so hard on. So, I set up a system whereby I require members of my board to participate in professionally prepared interviews so that my perspective is not skewed by my desire to help people. I have standard operating procedures in place so that I am doing the same research, questionnaires, and background checks on every person that I allow into any of my strong circles or businesses. Therefore, I cannot allow bias to dictate what my ultimate decision will be.

Like me, as individuals driven by a sense of purpose, you may find yourselves overlooking red flags when you genuinely like someone. There's a natural inclination to believe that our mission-driven nature can influence positive change or that we are somehow immune to potential harm due to a sense of ego. However, it's crucial to approach relationships with humility and a genuine understanding that no one is above misunderstandings or misjudgments.

In fostering empathy, let's strive to create spaces where our connections are based on mutual respect and understanding. By combining your courage to explore discomfort with a compassionate discernment coupled with systems to keep your decision making structured, you can build meaningful relationships that align with your values and contribute positively transforming your passion work into a fully funded business.

Call to Action:

Take a moment to reflect on your strong circle. Who are the individuals who define your success and provide you with strength and support? These relationships are the foundation of your journey, and they play a significant role in helping you reach your goals.

Focus on relationships, memberships, and strong circles and follow these steps to create your strong network:

1. Reflect on Your Current Network: Take a moment to assess your current network and relationships, both personally and professionally. Consider how these connections are influencing your journey and your mission-rich goals. Are they aligned with your values and objectives?

2. Identify Your Strong Circles: Think about the individuals who make up your strong circles. Who are the people providing you with support, guidance, and inspiration? Recognize their value in your life and mission.

3. Review Your Board and Team: If you're involved in a nonprofit or have a business, evaluate your board members and team. Are they aligned with your mission? Do they bring diverse skills and expertise that contribute to your goals? Consider any adjustments or additions needed.

4. Membership and Networks: If you're part of any memberships or networks, reflect on their impact. Are they providing you with valuable resources, support, and opportunities? Consider whether these memberships align with your mission and if you're maximizing their benefits.

5. Assess Your Delegating and Outsourcing Practices: Are you effectively leveraging the skills and talents of others? Are you maintaining integrity and authenticity in your business or mission-driven work?

6. Set Goals for Relationship Building: Establish specific goals for building and nurturing relationships. Whether it's expanding your strong circle, joining new memberships, or enhancing your team, having clear objectives will guide your actions.

7. Regularly Re-evaluate: Relationships, networks, and circles evolve. Commit to regular evaluations of these connections. Ensure they continue to align with your mission and provide the support you need.

8. Be Intentional and Authentic: As you expand and strengthen your network and teams, remain authentic to your values. Prioritize relationships that align with your mission and ensure that the people you delegate tasks to reflect your integrity.

9. Share Your Journey: Open up and share your journey with those who have supported you and those you support. Encourage a culture of growth and collaboration within your network and circles.

10. Invest in Your Network: Just as you invest in your business or mission, invest in your network, memberships, and teams. This may involve dedicating time, energy, or resources to ensure that these relationships thrive.

11. Seek Mentorship and Advice: If you're not sure where to start or how to enhance your relationships, seek mentorship or advice from those who have successfully built strong circles and teams.

12. Take Action: After reflecting and planning, take tangible steps to improve your network, memberships, and team. Whether it's reaching out to potential strong circle members or refining your delegation processes, action is key.

Building and nurturing strong relationships, memberships, and circles is not only essential but also an ongoing journey. By following this call-to-action plan, you can actively shape your network to better align with your mission-rich goals, support your authenticity and integrity, and ultimately achieve greater success. Your net worth truly is in alignment with your network, so make it a network that empowers your mission and aspirations.

CHAPTER SIX

Work & Life Balance

Time Thieves

Time thieves are insidious and often go unnoticed in our lives. We find ourselves at the end of the day, wondering why we didn't accomplish what we set out to do. The constant interruptions, whether it's the phone ringing, text messages popping up, or emails flooding our inbox, pull us away from our tasks. As leaders, we often feel an obligation to please and appease everyone, which can hinder our mission-rich work. We must learn to balance work and life to ensure we're taking care of ourselves, the ones responsible for leading the ship.

In my efforts to address this issue, I embarked on a journey of self-reflection by taking a close look at my daily habits. It became evident that I tended to respond to emails immediately, sometimes at the expense of other important tasks. Recognizing the need for change, I made the conscious decision to turn off email notifications and establish specific windows of time for checking my inbox. Additionally, I provided my assistant's contact information for genuine emergencies, assuring that

I could maintain my focus while remaining available for my staff and stakeholders when they truly needed me.

I also realized that social media had the potential to consume a significant portion of my day, often without me even realizing it. To mitigate this, I adopted Wormtools, a helpful tool that enabled me to implement a more structured approach to my social media use, ensuring that I wouldn't be drawn into it when more pressing matters demanded my attention.

However, I couldn't overlook the importance of empathy and understanding in my interactions with my children. Their "mommy, mommy" calls, though sometimes seemingly trivial, held great significance to them. In response, I set clear guidelines to minimize interruptions and ensure that my children's needs were met without compromising my ability to focus on my tasks. For example, during weekly family meetings I inform my children about important events that I have going on. Now that they're teens I can share the events from my Google calendar so that they do not forget when I cannot be interrupted with a phone call unless it's an emergency. They know that I can and will always check my phone for text messages and respond to those. I am clear with clients that I may have to respond to a text from my children during certain parts of the day. So, they know I will respond, but they also have limited their interruptions during the busiest times of my day.

When my children were younger, I brought them with me to events. They were my helpers – whether it was grabbing markers, putting up sticky paper, passing out copies. They had a job, and they took it very seriously. My businesses have always been a family affair. I pay them to work for me and I train them to assist me and all of them have embraced the entrepreneurial spirit.

Throughout this process, I learned that this was providing additional structure for my children while minimizing the guilt that I would experience knowing I needed to remain focused on my work responsibilities.

To combat time thieves effectively, we need to identify what steals our time throughout the day. Some use time chunks or planners, sticky notes, Google calendars, or traditional day planners to manage time. The key is to find a system that works for you, one that keeps you organized and on track. A sense of progress and accomplishment is essential to prevent burnout.

Purpose of Work-Life Balance in Business

Work-life balance is not just about work; for me, it is also about time for my family. Throughout my life as a mother and wife, my work has been centered around my faith, family, and desire to leave a legacy for our children. I worked with my husband to establish "business meetings" within our family to teach our children essential skills, such as Robert's Rules, minutes-taking, and agenda organization. These skills can be transferable to their future careers as leaders. In my case, I even employ my children in my business, allowing them to gain skills and experience.

Family

I have learned that family structure benefits our children and plays a crucial role in shaping us as parents and caregivers. When prioritized, it draws a level of consistency into our roles, requiring us to be authentic, whether at the grocery store, the office, in church, or at home. Drawing from my experience as a successful business leader, where I've thrived in assisting individuals beyond my household, the family structure allows us to integrate many effective techniques into our home life seamlessly.

Our family has used various tools with intentionality to impart the lessons learned to our children. These tools include family meetings, employing my children, creative discipline, and community engagement.

Family Meetings

Much like I've cultivated positive relationships in my professional journey without resorting to unethical practices, we stress the importance of the same principles to our children. Family meetings become a platform to instill these values, teaching them to navigate their lives with integrity and respect.

Incorporating our parenting skills into our professional lives is a subtle art that requires explanation. Inviting our children into these conversations imparts essential life skills and provides valuable insights for our professional development. The reciprocal nature of these discussions fosters a deeper understanding of navigating challenges at home and in the workplace.

Ultimately, family meetings serve as a platform for building positive relationships with our children, nurturing their growth, and instilling valuable business skills to serve them well as they transition into adulthood.

Employing Our Children

Our personal life challenges, such as budget management, generating income, and multitasking, equip us with transferable skills applicable to our business endeavors. Learning to delegate, seek reliable assistance, and balance time effectively are crucial for the success of your businesses and contribute to your family's prosperity.

I recognized parents' immense power in managing a family, often referring to it as "Mom Power" and "Dad Power." Managing a family underscores the transferability of skills needed to run a family to the business realm. Skills like budgeting, multitasking, negotiating, and maintaining a balanced schedule are transferable, and we should teach them to our children for personal and professional growth.

That is my primary reason for employing my children in my business. I teach them to be responsible, respect authority, make money, save money, and responsibly spend money. I also teach them firsthand the simplicity of running a business despite the complexities of the business world. "Train up a child..." as referenced in Proverbs 22:6, does not only refer to religious practices but also a mandate that will guide our children towards a path of success and good stewardship in all areas of their lives. They no longer frivolously spend our money; they are much more meticulous about spending their money.

Creative Discipline:

One of the primary responsibilities of a parent is to discipline their children. Like many parents, I made the mistake of equating discipline with punishment in my early years of motherhood. However, about a decade ago, I attended a conference where the speaker spoke about her mother's creative discipline methods. What I learned led me and my husband to create innovative discipline methods for our four children.

At the time of our shift to creative discipline, we had two children reading and writing in school and two that were not.

We wanted to teach our children how to learn from what they did, articulate why it was wrong, or advocate for themselves if they did not think it was wrong. The ones who could not write had to draw a photo, whereas the older ones could draw pictures but also had to write down their responses. We would also ask them to weigh in on the consequences of their actions, giving voice even if we ultimately came to a different conclusion.

As the years progressed, our children became avid writers and readers. They learned to do research, create presentations, and articulate their thoughts to advocate for themselves or an issue of interest to them. They have always been invited to participate in honors and AP-level math and English classes. A recent point of success is one of my children using these skills to secure a presidential scholarship covering her full tuition at a private college.

Community Engagement:

I never wanted to be the business leader who sacrificed my children for the greater good, as I witnessed happen to so many mission-focused families. Many of my mentors taught me not to make the same mistakes they did but to find a way to bring my children into the work. Therefore, as a practice, we have always involved our children in volunteer activities for our church, schools, and community. Volunteering to feed those hungry or giving away toys during the holidays is never optional; my children look forward to it. These experiences inspired them to take the initiative on their terms, leading to them receiving leadership awards for their civic and community service.

The other side of community engagement is receiving. I intentionally send my children to events offered by community organizations.

My children have learned about public speaking, teaching, entrepreneurship, art, music, and more through their involvement in community organizations. My children have already received recognition for their participation in youth development programs.

Effectiveness

Recognizing the significance of effectiveness has part of my personal journey. I've come to understand that taking on everything alone might not always be the most productive path. There's a certain vulnerability in admitting that I'm not an expert in every aspect of my work, like graphic design.

I found myself investing a considerable amount of time in creating flyers, only to realize that they lacked the impact I desired. I took some time to reflect and realized that I needed help to truly make a difference. So, I made the decision to bring in a professional graphic designer, investing $80 in their expertise.

The result went beyond just visually appealing flyers; it was a relief. I saved precious time, allowing me to redirect my energy towards a project that not only felt more fulfilling but also brought in $300. This experience taught me a profound lesson about the value of seeking help and focusing on what truly matters to be effective.

This journey of understanding effectiveness extended beyond graphic design. It was a pivotal lesson in my navigation of the complexities of my work, from managing finances to handling client meetings. Through it all, I've learned to approach challenges with empathy towards myself, acknowledging that seeking support isn't a sign of weakness but a pathway to growth.

I recognized that hiring an accountant and using tools like QuickBooks was an investment in my sanity and business. While it seemed costly at first, the time it saved me allowed for more family time, personal self-care, and business growth. These changes created space for quality moments with my spouse and family, helping me recharge and be more effective in my mission-rich work.

Efficiency

Moreover, I found that implementing efficient systems within my business allowed me to be more effective and free up valuable time. These systems helped me manage tasks and processes more efficiently, creating space for quality family time, personal self-care, or moments of relaxation with my spouse.

I remember when I started my LLC and did everything manually. I literally kept track of finances on spreadsheets, mileage in notebooks, and wrote manual checks for owner draws from my business account into my personal account. It was overwhelming but manageable when I was making a few thousand dollars a month. But, once my income started to increase, it became less manageable, and I had to find more automated methods to manage finances and administrative responsibilities.

I looked at the costs as part of the business process and factored the costs into my prices. Three things happened for me. First, I learned to streamline administrative tasks by employing software like Dubsado, and establishing strong organizational practices through standard operating procedures, and using mobile tools like Quickbooks. Second, I increased my profits because my business operations improved, and I could spend more time on the moneymaking part of my business.

Third, I provided myself with more time to unwind a nd s pend with loved ones.

Understand this, work-life balance is not just about time management; it's about protecting our time from time thieves and ensuring that our personal and family lives are in harmony with our business endeavors. By maintaining this balance, we can prevent burnout, strengthen our family bonds, and empower our businesses to thrive. Remember that a well-structured personal life is essential for an effective professional life. Strive to create a holistic approach that nurtures your personal life, family life, and business life to achieve the balance needed for success.

Setbacks can often lead us back into our old habits, especially when tragedy erupts in our lives. In times of crisis or personal challenges, we may unintentionally revert to less effective ways of managing our time, which highlights the importance of continuous self-awareness and discipline in maintaining our work-life balance.

So, I urge you to take a step back and assess your own life. Identify your time thieves, learn to delegate effectively, and implement systems that can free up your time for the things that truly matter – spending time with your family, nurturing your well-being, and rejuvenating your mind. In doing so, you'll not only achieve a better work-life harmony but also improve the vitality of your business and enjoy the rewards of a well-rounded, fulfilling life.

Learning the Hard Way

At the close of each day, it becomes unmistakably clear that the faces we return to in the evening are the ones that hold immeasurable significance. Whether these faces belong to our little ones, our life partners who share our home, or those individuals we hold dear outside our domestic walls or in our places of worship, they are the ones who truly matter. This realization struck home for millions, if not billions, during the enforced isolation of the COVID-19 pandemic.

On a deeply personal level, I experienced a profound awakening, as I previously described in an earlier chapter. I found myself on the edge of a nervous breakdown, burdened by the weight of others' problems, and attempting to shoulder a responsibility almost akin to that of a higher authority. I was battling with severe compassion fatigue caused by unhealthy emotional empathy.

The burnout I experienced was something that still haunts me. I can still feel the pain in my joints and muscles that started from my heart. It marked a pivotal juncture in my life where I had to muster my inner reserves of strength and assertiveness, setting clear boundaries, and adhering to them without wavering. I was resolute in my determination not to allow others to push me to the precipice of burnout once more. Moreover, I was steadfast in my commitment to avoid being drawn into a realm of bitterness or vengefulness, emotions that straddle the edge of enduring suffering.

I now understand with unwavering clarity that had this situation never occurred, I may have never been reborn. It took facing the reality that my strong why was in jeopardy because of the decisions I was making for me to stop, reflect, and redirect. I also know that there is no one here else capable of doing so in the way that I can. While my husband certainly contributes in his way, my approach tends to be distinct, driven by a unique perspective of nurturing and compassion. During these times of vulnerability, it becomes strikingly apparent that safeguarding our collective well-being and nurturing cherished relationships in our lives is not a mere indulgence but an undeniable necessity.

Finding Solutions

As I put into practice better strategies for balancing my work and life responsibilities, I realized that I had a lot of work to do as it related to building relationships with my children, husband, and others in my strong circle. We researched and read books, oftentimes as a family to improve upon our family infrastructure, communication, and relationships with one another.

I wanted to grow as a business leader, but I did not want to leave my children grappling against the walls of life. The family meetings helped to implement different strategies and identify tools to build a legacy. One of the tools we instituted to help solidify our foundation as a family was a family mission statement.

Family Mission Statement:

Sit down with your family and create a mission statement that reflects your shared values, goals, and priorities. This statement can serve as a guiding light in your personal and professional lives. Creating a family mission statement is a powerful tool for maintaining a harmonious work and life balance, especially when running a mission-rich business while imparting essential principles to your children. Here's a step-by-step guide on how to create one:

1. Gather the Family: Start by bringing your family together. Whether it's a weekly family meeting or a special session dedicated to this purpose, ensure that everyone is present and engaged.

2. Define Your Values: Discuss the values that are most important to your family. These can encompass personal and business values, such as integrity, compassion, hard work, and commitment to service.

3. Set Goals: Collaboratively, identify both short-term and long-term goals for your family. These can include personal goals like spending quality time together and business goals like making a positive impact on your community.

4. Craft Your Mission Statement: Summarize your values and goals into a concise and meaningful mission statement. Make it a reflection of your family's identity and purpose. For instance, "We are a family committed to serving our community through our mission-rich business while nurturing the bonds that strengthen us."

5. Discuss and Revise: Share the mission statement with your family and encourage open discussion. Allow everyone to express their thoughts, make suggestions, and propose revisions. Ensure that the final statement resonates with all family members.

6. Display and Live It: Once the mission statement is finalized, display it prominently in your home or workspace. Use it as a constant reminder of your family's shared values and objectives.

7. Practice What You Preach: As a family, strive to embody the principles outlined in your mission statement. Show your children, through your actions, how to balance work, life, and your mission-rich business effectively.

8. Regularly Revisit: Periodically revisit your family mission statement during your family meetings. Use it as a compass to evaluate your progress and make necessary adjustments to your work and life balance.

9. Teach Your Children: Explain the significance of the mission statement to your children and involve them in discussions about how it applies to both your family life and your mission-rich business.

By creating and embracing a family mission statement that encompasses your values, goals, and the importance of maintaining a healthy work and life balance, you'll not only run a successful mission-rich business but also instill essential life principles in your children, providing them with a strong foundation for their future endeavors.

Quality Family Bonding Time

Ensuring quality family bonding time is something I deeply value. I came across a study back in 2013 that highlighted the significance of family meals, demonstrating that having a family meal at least once a week can be a determining factor in whether a child develops substance addiction.

In my family, we've made it a tradition to dedicate at least one evening per week for a family meal where we can connect and bond. This cherished tradition not only enhances our family ties but also creates a space for meaningful discussions on important matters. If you can do more than one night a week, then you should do it and add regular date time with your spouse.

Nurturing Your Well-Being

It's vital to set aside dedicated time for self-care, mental and emotional rejuvenation, and faith. Whether it's indulging in a restorative weekly yoga class, immersing yourself in a captivating book during a quiet evening, or taking a staycation, these moments serve a dual purpose.

Not only does self-care contribute to personal well-being, but it's also the cornerstone of recharging and sustaining a flourishing mission-rich business.

If you're skeptical about the benefits of nurturing your well-being, consider trying to solve a complex issue before taking a break. Upon your return, revisit that challenge, and you'll be amazed at how swiftly creative solutions emerge or how you effortlessly recall the name of a person who can assist. Rest, or the lack of it, is a crucial determinant of effective progress, and combining it with faith and spiritual rejuvenation can further enhance your journey.

Personal Relationships:

It's essential to prioritize personal relationships beyond the realms of work and family. Actively nurture friendships and foster connections with others to ensure a well-rounded social life, which, in turn, contributes to the success of a profit-powered mission-rich business. I am not saying to make everyone your best friend, but I am saying that having someone to share the journey with makes it more rewarding. If you Google the importance of fostering connections, you will find that it is one of common threads among people who live long and healthy lives.

Conclusion: A Complete You is Better for Business

By embracing these measures to establish a healthy work/life balance will benefit those around you and extend to your business. You will embark on a journey toward a more harmonious and rewarding life. Here, your family, personal well-being, business, and spiritual growth can all flourish in unison. Furthermore, it creates a clear path for your children and mentees to follow, offering guidance on avoiding the less profitable road often linked with burnout due to financial constraints in running mission-rich businesses. It will teach them how to be mission-rich and profit-powered.

Call to Action:

Identify at least one aspect of balancing work and family life that was discussed in this chapter. Making the attempt to add all of these at once will not be productive or sustainable, but you should start with the one that will easiest to start with.

Implement weekly family meetings

Create a family mission statement

Employ your children in your business

Create a volunteer schedule for your family

Other: _____

CHAPTER SEVEN

Flawless Administration

Flawless Administration

We are now entering the most intricate section of the book. I deliberately placed this information toward the end because, despite being a crucial element of a business's foundation, it is akin to the skeleton of a body without flesh. Administration is what brings the business to life moving it from passion work or a hobby into a business. It provides the vessels for income and expenses to flow, and holds the important aspects of the business such as finances, marketing, human resources, goals, and planning. In simpler terms, how you present yourself and how others perceive your brand can have a more significant impact on your profitability than most of the topics we'll go deeper in the upcoming chapters.

However, it's the combination of technical and operational aspects, both influenced by the human factor, that ultimately determines the success of your mission-driven business. Patience is key here; it will save you a considerable amount of time, frustration, and money.

I've come to realize that impeccable administration and a robust business infrastructure serve as the bedrock of a successful mission-driven venture. It's essential to understand that "impeccable" doesn't equate to perfection. Instead, it signifies that, in the event of an IRS audit, your diligent effort to adhere to the laws to the best of your knowledge is evident. It's about establishing a record that demonstrates your commitment to doing the right thing, even when it might not appear that way on the surface.

So, what are the fundamental requirements for a legitimate business structure? Whether you're pursuing a 501(c)(3) organization, a single-member LLC, or any other type of entity, certain rules apply. You need to meet specific criteria to be recognized as a legal entity by both the Internal Revenue Service and your state or commonwealth. Understanding the tax codes, such as the 501(c)(3) designation, is crucial to your journey. Most people are unaware of why it's called 501(c)(3), and I'll shed light on this.

When it comes to single-member LLCs, often considered disregarded entities, it's important to know why you should file them on your Schedule C. While some might choose to treat their single-member LLC as an S-Corp, we'll focus less on this strategy. Much of what I'm sharing applies to both approaches. So, whether you're starting a nonprofit, an LLC, or a corporation, it's crucial to define your mission, outline your programs and services, and demonstrate the need for your work.

Every business, mission-rich or not, must have an executive summary, identify the target demographic, articulate its mission and vision, estimate the required funding, and budget for salaries. Even if you're deeply passionate about your mission, you can't assume that people will volunteer their time indefinitely. Understand that volunteer time has value, and expecting everything for free is not a sustainable approach. Independentsector.org has a list of the value of the volunteer hour in each state. Nothing is free! Everything and everyone has a value and that value can be and should be notated in your annual budget, even when in-kind.

Your budget tells the story of your business. It will indicate what you value most and whether you have a realistic gauge of what it takes to run a business. It is one thing to not have salaries in your budget, but most mission-rich individuals will not have a line item for your own salary. You are the most important asset to your organization, but you forget that the "worker is worthy of his (or her) wages worthy of their reward" when it comes to your work. (I Timothy 5:18) You cannot continue to work for free and take money from your personal accounts to fund your business as a sustainable funding model. (That only works when you are very wealthy and donate money from a for-profit entity into a nonprofit such as a family foundation).

For ALL entities, funding is essential for sustainability. If you want to be taken seriously and attract real funders, you must follow certain guidelines. I often meet people with grand visions of starting businesses focused on empowering and helping people, but they're not prepared for the responsibilities and the need for structured, systematic administration. This often shows up in the finance and annual reports when the profit and loss statements do not match the income statements and the general ledger is missing vital information or annual reports have not been filed.

A Missed Opportunity

I vividly remember the day I had the opportunity to meet with a generous multi-millionaire. I was able to convince him to join me and my supervisor for a lunch meeting. His interest in funding our project seemed apparent, but he did not request a budget or anything in writing.

In our eagerness, we went to that meeting thinking it was a chance to engage in a casual conversation. And we did just that—talked and shared our aspirations. However, in hindsight, our actions subtly conveyed that we were not adequately prepared for the next crucial step. To be honest, we weren't.

It was a turning point because that very same individual went on to fund another organization with a mission that mirrored ours but with a meticulously planned and well-structured approach. Today, that organization has flourished into a multi-million-dollar venture, complete with a school. We, unfortunately, missed that opportunity.

This experience has left a lasting impact on me, reminding me of the significance of readiness and the importance of being fully prepared when these unique opportunities arise. It's a lesson learned with a touch of empathy, knowing that we all have moments where we miss out, but those moments can serve as valuable stepping stones to growth and future success.

Be careful when you roll with the rumor mill that an organization just "got" funded. It's rare for a dysfunctional and disorganized organization to receive large amounts of funding in its early years. It's rarer for an organization to sustain beyond the grant term if they somehow access the funds in the first place.

Structure is Vital

An organization's structure is paramount. I've prepared an organizational chart for profitable nonprofit businesses, but it's important to note that each nonprofit may have unique structures based on its bylaws and articles of incorporation. You need a budget, a strategic plan, and a business plan to attract funders, and it's vital to provide statistics and differentiate your work from others in the same field.

Whether you choose a non-profit or for-profit path, understand that there's a significant difference between the interests of nonprofit funders and for-profit investors. Your structure and approach should align with your goals and work ethic. Before diving in, assess your preferences and work ethic, and ensure they align with your chosen structure.

It's also essential to understand that mission-rich projects don't always have to be standalone organizations. Fiscal sponsorship is an option, allowing you to apply for grant funding without a 501(c)3 status, and funds pass through your fiscal sponsor. However, this path comes with risks, such as the possibility of your idea being taken or misappropriated.

The corporate mindset is vital in non-profit leadership and combining it with mission-rich goals can lead to a successful business. Systems, deadlines, and structure are equally crucial in both corporate and non-profit environments. You should never treat your mission-rich venture as a charity; it should be a serious business. Successful leaders prioritize time for strategic growth and development, and it's essential to set aside dedicated time to work on your business, not just in it.

Administration may seem tedious, but it sets you apart from others and enhances your ability to fulfill your mission. Most non-profits neglect administration, and this affects their credibility. To attract substantial funding and build a sustainable legacy, you must take your administration seriously.

Tax Codes You Need to Know

It's crucial to understand that the tax code, often perceived as complex and intimidating, can become your trusted guide on the path to building a legacy of wealth. Rather than being afraid of it, consider the tax code as a sort of "business bible" – a comprehensive resource designed to help you ensure the profitability and sustainability of your entity.

The tax code offers an array of provisions and strategies that can significantly benefit your business. Let's explore some key resources within the tax code that can serve as invaluable references.

1. Tax Publication 583 - Starting a Business and Keeping Records: This publication is like your startup's compass. It provides essential guidance on how to initiate your business endeavors, maintain meticulous records, and establish a strong foundation.

2. Tax Publication 535 - Business Expenses: Think of this publication as your ledger of possibilities. It details the array of business expenses you can deduct, which can have a substantial impact on your overall profitability.

3. Tax Publication 587 - Home Office Deduction: If you run your business from home, this publication becomes your treasure map. It leads you through the process of claiming deductions related to your home office and unlocking valuable tax benefits.

4. Tax Publication 15, Circular E - Employer's Tax Guide: This guide is your roadmap for the strategic hiring of family employees. It instructs you on the steps to take and the considerations to make when bringing family members into your business, ensuring you make the most of this potential opportunity.

5. Code 501(c)3: This section of the tax code is your ultimate reference for nonprofit organizations. It offers specific guidelines for obtaining tax-exempt status and maintaining your nonprofit's compliance with the IRS, reinforcing the importance of adhering to these regulations for long-term success.

The tax code is more than a collection of rules and regulations – it's a valuable resource that, when understood and utilized correctly, can significantly impact your business's financial health. By leveraging these provisions and tax publications, you're not only ensuring that you're on the right side of the law, but you're also optimizing your profitability and securing the legacy of wealth you aspire to build.

Don't shy away from the tax code; embrace it as your partner in achieving financial success and long-term sustainability for your entity. But remember the IRS tax code is federal. There are varying tax regulations within your state.

BEWARE of the fads of creating your business in a state other than where you live. I will share more about this in a later chapter, but it can work against you in the long run if you do not actually do business in that other state.

Running a Legal and Legit Business

Let's emphasize the importance of being considered a legal entity in your home state and according to the IRS for various business structures, including nonprofit organizations, LLCs (Limited Liability Companies), sole proprietorships, and S-Corporations:

Non-profit Organization:

- For non-profit organizations, achieving legal entity status in your home state is a foundational step. This typically involves registering with the appropriate state authorities and adhering to state-specific nonprofit regulations.

- Obtaining 501(c)3 status from the IRS is a critical step for nonprofit legal recognition at the federal level. This designation not only exempts your organization from federal income taxes but also allows donors to make tax-deductible contributions.

Limited Liability Company (LLC):

- Forming an LLC is the process of creating a legal entity recognized by your home state. It provides limited liability protection to its owners (members) and ensures that the business operates as a distinct legal entity separate from its owners.

- While LLCs have flexibility in how they are taxed, they must still meet the legal requirements of their home state and the IRS to maintain their status.

Sole Proprietorship:

- A sole proprietorship is the simplest business structure but is not a separate legal entity from its owner. The owner and the business are considered one and the same in the eyes of the law.

- Compliance with state and local business regulations is essential for ensuring that your sole proprietorship is a legal entity in your home state. This includes permits and licenses required by your locality.

S-Corporation (S-Corp):

- Registering as an S-Corporation establishes your business as a legal entity in your home state, separating it from the individual owners (shareholders).

- S-Corps must adhere to strict IRS requirements to maintain their legal status, including limitations on the number and type of shareholders, meeting specific tax and reporting obligations, and more.

In all cases, whether it's a nonprofit organization, an LLC, a sole proprietorship, or an S-Corporation, being recognized as a legal entity in your home state is crucial. This recognition ensures that you can conduct business activities, enter contracts, own property, and enjoy the legal protections and obligations associated with your chosen business structure. Compliance with IRS regulations is also vital, as it impacts your tax status, which can significantly affect your financial health and sustainability.

Maintaining legal entity status at both the state and federal levels is not only a legal requirement but also essential for the credibility, sustainability, and success of your mission-rich venture or business. Be sure to consult with legal and tax professionals to ensure you're meeting all state and federal legal and regulatory requirements.

Now, let's explore the basic descriptions, pros, and cons of various business structures in Table 1 on page 96 and Table 2 on page 97.

Business Structures, Pros, Cons, & Taxes

Structure	Pros	Cons	Tax Requirements
Single Member LLC: combines limited liability protection with simplified taxation for single owners.	• Limited liability: Personal assets are protected. • Simplicity: Fewer formalities. • Pass-through taxation: Business income on the owner's tax return.	• Limited growth potential. • Self-employment taxes apply.	**Federal Tax:** By default, single-member LLCs are taxed as sole proprietorships. The business income is reported on the owner's individual tax return (Form 1040). The LLC itself does not pay federal income taxes. **Self-Employment Tax:** Owners are typically required to pay self-employment taxes, which cover Social Security and Medicare, on their share of the LLC's profits. **State Taxes:** State tax requirements can vary, but most states follow a similar pass-through taxation approach. Some states may impose additional LLC taxes or fees.
Partnership LLC: involves multiple owners sharing responsibilities	• Shared decision-making. • Pass-through taxation. • Limited liability.	• Potential for conflicts. • Complex profit-sharing.	**Federal Tax:** Like single-member LLCs, partnership LLCs do not pay federal income taxes. Profits and losses pass through to the individual partners, who report this on their individual tax returns (Form 1065). **Self-Employment Tax:** Partners are usually subject to self-employment tax on their share of profits. **State Taxes:** State tax requirements for partnership LLCs are similar to those for single-member LLCs.
S-Corporation: offers limited liability and pass-through taxation to shareholders.	• Limited liability. • Avoids double taxation. • Attracts investors.	• Strict eligibility criteria. • Complex regulations.	**Federal Tax:** S-Corporations offer pass-through taxation, meaning the business itself does not pay federal income tax. Instead, shareholders report their share of profits and losses on their individual tax returns (Form 1120S). **Self-Employment Tax:** Shareholders who actively participate in the business are required to pay self-employment taxes only on their salaries, not on profits. **State Taxes:** State tax requirements for S-Corporations can vary, but they typically follow a pass-through model

Table 1

Business Structures, Pros, Cons, & Taxes

Problem	Pros	Cons	Tax Requirements
Sole-Propietorship: a single-owner, unincorporated business	• Simplicity. • Full control. • Direct tax benefits.	• No liability protection.	**Federal Tax:** Sole proprietors report business income and expenses on their individual tax returns (Form 1040, Schedule C). The business itself does not pay federal income taxes. **Self-Employment Tax:** Sole proprietors are responsible for paying self-employment taxes on their net earnings, which cover Social Security and Medicare. **State Taxes:** State tax requirements for sole proprietorships are similar to those for other individual filers.
Nonprofit: focus on charitable, educational, or religious purposes.	• Tax-exempt status. • Tax-deductible donations. • Social impact.	• Limited revenue sources. • Regulatory compliance. • Limited profit distribution.	**Federal Tax:** Nonprofits are eligible to apply for tax-exempt status under Section 501(c) of the Internal Revenue Code. If approved, they are exempt from federal income taxes. However, they are still required to file annual information returns (Form 990) with the IRS. **State Taxes:** Nonprofits may be eligible for state tax exemptions, but requirements vary by state. Many states have their own reporting and compliance requirements for nonprofits.
501c3: tax-exempt nonprofit eligible for tax-deductible contributions.	• Tax exemption. • Attracts donations. • Credibility.	• Stringent eligibility. • Limited revenue activities. • Restrictions on political involvement.	**Federal Tax:** A 501(c)(3) organization is a specific type of nonprofit eligible for federal tax exemption. It does not pay federal income taxes. It must file Form 990 annually to maintain its tax-exempt status. **State Taxes:** Like other nonprofits, 501(c)(3) organizations may be eligible for state tax exemptions. State requirements and reporting vary.

Table 2

These structures offer different benefits and challenges, so your choice should align with your specific goals and resources. Consult with professionals to make an informed decision.

Tax requirements can change over time and may also depend on the specific activities and income of your business or organization. It's important to stay informed about federal and state tax regulations and consult with a tax professional to ensure compliance.

Let's discuss the importance of not granting full autonomy to anyone outside your organization and provide some suggested questions to ask accountants to ensure accountability and transparency.

The Importance of Maintaining Control:

Maintaining control over your business or organization is crucial for various reasons:

1. Accountability: When you retain control, you can ensure that your organization's finances, operations, and decisions align with your mission and values. Full autonomy may lead to actions that contradict your objectives.

2. Transparency: Keeping control allows you to maintain transparency with stakeholders, donors, and supporters. It's essential to maintain their trust and demonstrate your commitment to your mission.

3. Legal Responsibility: As the owner or leader of an organization, you bear legal responsibility for its actions. Granting full autonomy to external parties can complicate legal matters and make it challenging to protect your interests.

4. Mission Alignment: Your mission-driven organization exists to fulfill a specific purpose. Retaining control ensures that every action and decision is in harmony with your mission.

5. Risk Mitigation: Outsourcing control can expose your organization to additional risks, such as financial mismanagement or reputational damage. Maintaining control allows you to mitigate and address these risks effectively.

Suggested Questions for Accountants

When working with an accountant, it's crucial to ask the right questions to ensure they understand your organization's mission and values and are committed to maintaining transparency and accountability. Here are some suggested questions:

1. Can you explain your experience with nonprofit accounting? - This question helps gauge the accountant's familiarity with the unique financial and reporting requirements of nonprofit organizations.

2. What steps will you take to ensure compliance with all tax regulations applicable to our organization? - It's essential to confirm that the accountant is committed to keeping your organization in full compliance with tax laws.

3. How do you handle financial reporting for nonprofits, and can you provide examples of your past work with similar organizations? - This question assesses their ability to produce accurate and transparent financial reports.

4. What is your approach to ensuring the financial health and sustainability of our organization? - This question helps determine if the accountant is proactive in identifying financial challenges and proposing solutions.

5. How will you ensure transparency in our financial transactions and reporting? - Transparency is essential for maintaining trust with stakeholders, so understanding the accountant's approach is crucial.

6. Can you provide references from other nonprofit organizations you've worked with in the past? - Contacting references allows you to verify the accountant's track record and reliability.

7. What are your contingency plans in case of unforeseen financial challenges or audits? - A good accountant should have strategies in place to handle unexpected financial issues or audits effectively.

8. How do you keep up to date with changing tax laws and financial regulations that may affect our organization? - Staying informed about legal changes is crucial for compliance.

9. Can you describe your approach to budgeting and financial planning for nonprofits? - An accountant's approach to budgeting can significantly impact an organization's financial stability.

10. How do you prioritize maintaining the organization's mission and values in financial decision-making? - This question ensures the accountant understands the importance of aligning financial decisions with your mission.

By asking these questions and carefully selecting an accountant with the right experience and commitment to your mission-driven organization, you can maintain control, transparency, and accountability, while ensuring your financial affairs are managed effectively.

Checklist for Starting a Business

Starting a business, whether it's a nonprofit organization, a for-profit venture, or a mission-driven project, is an exciting and impactful journey. I'd like to offer you a checklist of essential items and steps you need to take to set the foundation for your new venture. Remember, this journey is not only about your vision but also about creating a structure that will support your mission and goals.

Business Start-up Checklist

1. Vision and Mission Statement: - Your vision and mission statements are the heart and soul of your venture. They define your purpose and values. Take the time to craft clear, inspiring statements that resonate with your objectives.

2. Legal Structure: - Choose the right legal structure for your business. This could be a single-member LLC, a partnership LLC, an S-corporation, a sole proprietorship, a nonprofit organization, or a 501(c)3 entity. Select the one that aligns with your goals and values.

3. Business Plan: - Develop a comprehensive business plan. Outline your objectives, strategies, and financial projections. A well-thought-out plan is your roadmap to success.

4. Register Your Business: - Register your business with the appropriate state or local authorities. This step makes your business officially recognized and compliant with local regulations.

5. Employer Identification Number (EIN): - Obtain an EIN from the IRS if you plan to have employees or if your business structure requires it. This unique identifier is crucial for tax purposes and financial transactions.

6. Business Bank Account: - Open a separate bank account for your business. This ensures your personal and business finances remain distinct, simplifying accounting and tax reporting.

7. Permits and Licenses: - Check local, state, and federal requirements for permits and licenses. Compliance is essential to avoid legal issues down the road.

8. Accounting and Bookkeeping System: - Set up an accounting and bookkeeping system that suits your business structure. Keeping accurate financial records is essential for transparency and compliance.

9. Budget and Financial Planning: - Create a budget and financial plan. This helps you manage your finances, allocate resources effectively, and ensure financial sustainability.

10. Insurance: - Consider the insurance needs of your business. Depending on your activities, you might need liability insurance, property insurance, or other forms of coverage.

11. Website and Online Presence: - Establish a website and create a strong online presence. In today's digital age, this is often the first point of contact with potential supporters or customers.

12. Fundraising and Donor Management System: - If you're a non-profit or mission-driven entity, implement a system for fundraising and donor management. This will help you track contributions and maintain strong relationships with supporters.

13. Compliance with Tax Regulations: - Ensure you understand and comply with tax regulations specific to your business structure. Non-profit organizations, for example, have unique tax obligations.

14. Human Resources: - If you plan to hire employees, set up HR processes, including payroll, benefits, and personnel policies.

15. Record Keeping: - Establish a system for record-keeping. This includes maintaining copies of important documents, contracts, and financial records.

16. Mission Focus: - Never lose sight of your mission and values. These principles should guide every decision you make and every action you take.

Starting a business is an intricate process, but each step brings you closer to your mission and goals. Remember, every successful organization starts with a vision and a plan. Stay focused, remain flexible, and be open to learning along the way. Your commitment to your mission-rich venture is commendable, and I'm here to support you every step of the way. If you ever have questions or need guidance, don't hesitate to reach out. Wishing you a successful and purposeful journey!

Let's identify which steps and components relate to nonprofit organizations, LLCs (Limited Liability Companies), and sole proprietorships. This information is also outlined in Table 3 on page 104.

Special Note on S-Corporations (S-Corp):

S-corporations are a specific type of business structure that combines limited liability protection with pass-through taxation. Like other business structures, they need to have a clear vision, register with the appropriate authorities, maintain separate financial accounts, manage permits and licenses, and keep meticulous financial records. Additionally, S-Corps must adhere to specific IRS eligibility criteria and compliance requirements to maintain their status.

As you embark on your journey to build a mission-rich and profit-powered legacy, remember that the path to success is paved with intention, planning, and unwavering dedication. Your commitment to making a positive impact in the world is commendable, and the steps you take today will shape a better future.

Business Start-up Table

Requirement	Sole-Proprietor	Single-Member LLC	S-Corp LLC	Nonprofit
Vision and Mission Statement	Only if you are Mission-Rich	Only if you are Mission-Rich	Only if you are Mission-Rich	
Legal Structure	No			
Business Plan	Recommended	Recommended	Recommended	
Register Your Business	No			
Employer Identification Number (EIN)	Depends on Preference or Hiring Employees			
Business Bank Account	Optional			
Permits and Licenses	Depends	Depends	Depends	Depends
Accounting and Bookkeeping System	Recommended			
Budget and Financial Planning	Recommended			
Insurance	No	Recommended	Recommended	Recommended
Website and Online Presence	Depends	Recommended	Recommended	Recommended
Fundraising and Donor Management System	No	No	No	
Compliance with Tax Regulations				
Human Resources	No	Depends	Depends	Depends
Record Keeping				
Mission Focus	Only if you are Mission-Rich	Only if you are Mission-Rich	Only if you are Mission-Rich	

Table 3

Conclusion: Bringing it All Together

There is a lot of work that must be done to ensure that your business is structured properly, but it is the work that is often overlooked because it is not fun unless you enjoy administrative work. I do not expect you to commit to doing all of this work by yourself although many of you will initially try and then fail.

It is vital for you to know what needs to be done so that you can be informed enough to know if the individuals you hire to do this work for you know what they are doing. However, it is not in the best interest of your entity for you to do all of the work yourself on a long-term basis.

Call to Action:

Now that you have come to terms with what what needs to be done, I want you to do the following:

Think about where you are in your business.

Ask yourself which aspects of the checklists and tables are foreign to you?

Which aspects of the guidelines are non-existent in your business?

Write down what you need for your business?

Visit Monroenaylor.com for your free Flawless Admin-istration assessment tool.

Remember, building a mission-rich and profit-powered legacy is not just about the destination; it's about the journey you embark on today. Your commitment to creating a lasting impact is a beacon of hope in our world.

If you ever need further guidance or have questions along the way, I'm here to support you. Your mission-rich venture deserves to thrive, and together, we can make it happen.

CHAPTER EIGHT

Planning & Strategy

Crafting a Vision for Success

Welcome to the realm of planning and strategy, where we embark on the journey of dissecting the ideals behind our mission-rich ventures. It's paramount that we not only identify our activatable passion – the burning desire that fuels our mission, our bankable time, and our capacity to balance work and life, all while delivering with excellence and empathy – but also learn how to sustain and fund our mission. To accomplish this, we must embrace unconventional brainstorming methods.

When I started my non-profit organization, I organized a community brainstorming session that involved over 80 diverse participants from various backgrounds, professions, and ages. This session, coupled with focus groups and surveys, allowed us to identify gaps in our community and design programs tailored to those needs. Too often, well-intentioned individuals dive into mission-rich work without fully understanding the true needs of their audience. This can lead to perceived needs that don't align with reality.

To succeed, we must engage in thorough research, brainstorming, focus groups, and even offer free sessions or product samples to gauge real interest and needs. Understanding the true needs is just the beginning – then comes the task of marketing, messaging, and framing our offerings to resonate with our target audience.

So, how does this tie into our funding strategies? It all boils down to establishing credibility. When you embark on your mission-rich venture, be it nonprofit or for-profit, you'll encounter various stakeholders who'll ask the same essential questions: Who do you serve? Why do you serve them? How do you know your work is effective in addressing their needs? Thus, your planning is a critical element in building a strong and fundable foundation.

Here are some vital steps in preparing your venture for the world of funding:

Strategic Tips for a Successful Mission-Rich Venture:

Alignment with Purpose:	Ensure that every strategic decision aligns with your mission and values. Regularly evaluate whether your actions are contributing to your overarching purpose.
Adaptive Planning:	Create a flexible strategic plan that can adapt to changing circumstances and opportunities. Being open to adjustments can make your venture more resilient.
Community Involvement:	Involve your community and supporters in your strategic planning. They can provide valuable insights, feedback, and resources to help your mission thrive.
Data-Driven Decisions:	Utilize data and analytics to make informed decisions. Collect data on the impact of your work and use it to improve your strategies.

Partnerships and Collaboration:	Seek strategic partnerships with organizations that share your mission or can complement your efforts. Collaboration can amplify your impact.
Diversified Funding:	Explore multiple sources of funding to reduce financial risks. Don't rely on a single funding stream. This might include grants, donations, earned revenue, and more.
Long-Term Vision:	Keep your long-term vision in mind while addressing short-term challenges. A clear vision will guide your strategic choices and provide motivation.
Impact Assessment:	Regularly assess the impact of your work on your target demographic. This helps you fine-tune your strategies and communicate your achievements effectively.
Advocacy and Awareness:	Use advocacy and awareness campaigns strategically to build support for your mission. An engaged community can help advance your goals.
Professional Development:	Invest in professional development for you and your team. Gaining new skills and knowledge can improve the execution of your mission.
Feedback Loops:	Establish feedback loops with your audience, donors, and supporters. Regular feedback can guide improvements in your offerings and strategies.
Crisis Preparedness:	Develop a crisis management plan to handle unexpected challenges. Being prepared can help you navigate difficult times more effectively.
Monitoring and Evaluation:	Implement a system for ongoing monitoring and evaluation of your activities. It's crucial for continuous improvement and transparency.
Scalability Planning:	If you aim for growth, plan for scalability from the beginning. Ensure your systems and processes can handle increased demand without compromising quality.
Celebrate Milestones:	Celebrate your achievements and milestones along the way. Acknowledging progress boosts morale and motivates your team and supporters.

These strategic tips can provide a strong foundation for your mission-rich venture. Remember, strategic planning is an ongoing process, and staying adaptable and committed to your mission is key to long-term success. If you ever need assistance with any aspect of your venture, feel free to reach out. Your dedication to creating a positive impact in the world is truly inspiring.

As you venture forward, consider the words from Luke 14:28: "For which of you, intending to build a tower, sitteth not down first and counteth the cost, whether he has sufficient to finish it?" It's a reminder that wise planning and a comprehensive strategy are the keys to success. Don't leave your business endeavors unfinished; honor the commitment that has been placed in your heart.

Grant Writing Versus Grant Strategy

When you talk to somebody and say you want a grant writer, you are subject to hiring somebody who will fill out an application and submit it, with the sole goal of securing funding by any means necessary. This is often because you've likely negotiated with them that they will only get paid if you obtain the grant. However, a professional grant writer operates differently. They don't merely see themselves as grant writers but as stewards of the work they undertake. They hold integrity in high regard and strive to ensure that whatever they include in the application is something you can genuinely achieve and deliver through the funds you're requesting. Whether it's funding for a program, services, or products, they aim to make sure you can fulfill your commitment.

This is where the grant strategy comes into play. To formulate a grant strategy, you not only need your administration in order and your administrative infrastructure to be well-structured, but you must also have a plan for growth and sustainability. It's about understanding how a specific grant application aligns with your mission and fits into your larger vision. It's crucial to recognize that all money isn't good money, and not all grants are the right fit for your organization.

A grant is essentially a contract, meaning you're obligated to deliver the services or products you committed to when you accept the funding. Relying on someone who's only focused on getting the grant may lead to them including elements in the grant application that aren't aligned with your true goals or capacity.

To operate with integrity, you should prioritize a grant strategy over a grant writing approach. By doing so, you'll be more valuable to your funders because, when you sit down with them, you'll present a multi-layered approach to how you plan to utilize their funding. This approach includes strategies for leveraging the grant funds to secure additional funding and generate profits, all while ensuring the sustainability of your organization or entity. This commitment to a strategic approach not only enhances your credibility but also helps you maintain the integrity of your mission-rich venture.

Funding Strategy – The Ultimate Goal

Another invaluable lesson that I'd like to emphasize is that a funding strategy is far more comprehensive than a grant strategy. Keep the grant strategy as an aspect of the funding strategy. Many individuals may gravitate towards grant writing because it seems more straightforward, there's a persistent myth that securing grants should be their primary goal. However, this mindset overlooks the importance of having a well-thought-out strategy in place to ensure grant success.

Without a strategy you will have a bunch of beautifully written grant applications sitting in a funder's portal or on their desk.

In my experience, I've found that having a robust strategy is the key to achieving funding goals. Over the years, I've written numerous grant applications, ranging from modest $5,000 grants to substantial $1.5 million grants. Remarkably, an impressive 95 to 98 percent of the grants I've written have been successfully funded. This high success rate is a testament to the power of strategic thinking over mere grant writing.

The distinction lies in the fact that I don't chase dollars; instead, I focus on attracting like-hearted funders who believe in the vision I'm presenting, who resonate with the services I provide, and who genuinely want to fund the work I am passionate about. This approach is what sets the foundation for sustainability and profitability in any mission-rich venture.

Every time I've succeeded in obtaining six or seven-figure funding, it's been because I entered the funding application process with a comprehensive plan. I took the time to meet with the funders and fully understand their expectations, financial considerations, and the value they place on specific aspects. This approach held true whether I was working on behalf of an LLC or a nonprofit organization.

Another aspect to this is doing your research. Learn what the trending phrases are and do your best to stay relevant in how you communicate what you do to your funders. Here is an example of how you can say the same thing but have create more of an impact using an empathetic and culturally responsive mission statement:

1. Sample Mission Statement - We help homeless teens get housing.

2. Sample Mission Statement - We are committed to providing teens who are homeless with a place to live and belong so that they are empowered to rebuild their lives and discover their full potential.

In sum, the lesson here is clear: while grant writing plays a part, it's the overall strategy that ultimately leads to success in securing funding. Your success story, whether in a for-profit or nonprofit context, is more likely when you approach funding with a holistic, multi-layered strategy that encompasses your vision and objectives. This approach ensures not only the financial support you need but also the lasting impact and sustainability of your mission-rich endeavor.

Incorporate Networking into Your Funding Strategy

One vital aspect of a successful funding strategy is selfless engagement within your professional networks. When you actively contribute to your network, you become more visible and form genuine connections with like-hearted individuals and organizations. This visibility and authenticity can significantly benefit your mission-rich venture, especially when linked to your funding strategy.

Engaging with legislators and local officials can also widen your reach and impact. When these key figures see your work and recognize your effectiveness, empathy, and authenticity, they are more likely to support your efforts. They prefer working with individuals who genuinely care about making a difference and have a track record of achieving positive outcomes. This is where your commitment to your mission, your passion, and your focus on excellence with empathy come into play.

By cultivating relationships with these influential stakeholders, you can tap into additional funding opportunities and resources. They can advocate for your cause, connect you with potential funders, and open doors to partnerships that align with your mission. The support and credibility gained through such engagements can further enhance your funding strategy by diversifying your sources of financial support and strengthening your organization's reputation.

Let's not start businesses and leave them incomplete. Your mission is a divine calling that must be fulfilled. It's a relentless drive that won't let you rest until you've accomplished it. Your call to action: Create an executive summary and a concise business plan or action plan to bring your mission to life.

Funding Strategy is also About People

Why is it crucial to disrupt fear caused by our comfort zone and intentionally focus on leadership, trauma-informed communication, empathetic listening, and diverse personality style training to be successful in implementing an effective funding strategy? Because, as a business leader, you are always in the people business, whether you realize it or not. Even if you hire someone else to focus on fundraising and finance, you are, in essence, the chief fundraiser for your organization. This is a fundamental truth that often goes overlooked.

You see, your mission-rich venture doesn't exist in a vacuum. It's intertwined with the lives, hopes, and experiences of real people – your team, your beneficiaries, your supporters, and your partners. To succeed in this complex ecosystem, you must be equipped with not just technical skills but a profound understanding of human dynamics and relationships.

Leadership skills are essential because they allow you to guide your team and your mission. Trauma-informed approaches help you relate to the experiences of those you serve, recognizing that many have undergone significant challenges. Effective communication is vital to articulate your vision, inspire your team, and connect with your supporters. Empathetic listening deepens your understanding of others and fosters trust and collaboration. Understanding diverse personality styles enables you to tailor your interactions, knowing that one size doesn't fit all.

All these elements form the bedrock of your mission's success. Your venture's mission is not just about a goal; it's about the people you impact. When you focus on leadership, trauma-informed approaches, communication, empathetic listening, and understanding diverse personality styles, you become better equipped to serve those people effectively and create genuine connections.

Now, how does this tie into your funding strategies? Well, when you prioritize these skills and approaches, you're more likely to attract funders, partners, and supporters who align with your values. Your authenticity, your commitment to understanding and empathizing with others, and your ability to communicate your mission effectively make you an attractive leader for your organization. People are naturally drawn to individuals who not only have a compelling mission but also possess the interpersonal skills to bring it to life.

In a world where human connection is often overlooked, these skills set you apart and enable you to establish meaningful relationships with stakeholders. Whether you're engaging with potential funders, partners, or supporters, your ability to connect on a human level creates the trust and rapport that underpin successful funding strategies.

So, as you venture forward on your mission-rich path, consider that understanding the human element is just as important as crafting a winning strategy. Your call to action is to create an executive summary and a concise business plan or action plan, infused with the skills and approaches mentioned earlier, embodying your vision and strategy. By doing so, you set the course for a brighter and more impactful future. This segues right into our final chapter, exiting the road less profitable and entering the state of profit-powered.

Call To Action:

Your business action and concise business plans are essential starting points for your strategic planning process. A concise business plan aims to convey your business idea effectively and efficiently. Therefore, avoid unnecessary jargon or lengthy explanations and focus on key information highlighting your business's potential for success. Your business action plan intends to clarify critical steps you need to take to bring your entity to a place of sustainability.

Visit monroenaylor.com for a templates to simpli-fy placement and funding planning for your business such as Concise Business Plan and Business Action Plan worksheets.

Dollars Can Follow You

Chapter Nine: Paving the Way to Profit Power

As we embark on this final chapter, it's essential to reflect on the journey we've taken together so far. We've explored the intricate world of mission-rich entities, both for-profit and nonprofit, unraveling misconceptions and shedding light on the hurdles that often stand in the way of successful business startups. We've ventured beyond our comfort zones and discovered the immense value of leading with authenticity and empathy. We've unpacked the significance of building robust relationships, fostering memberships, maintaining a work-life balance, and the art of flawless administration, all while crafting an effective plan and strategy for our ventures.

Now, we stand at the threshold of the profit-powered state, the culmination of all our efforts and learning. This chapter is devoted to understanding funding, eligibility, and the vital infrastructure needed to transform your mission-rich organization into a credible and fundable entity.

Remember that motivation for funding your entity differ depending on the type of entity you are establishing.

Tax deductibility + MISSION =
motivation for individuals to fund a nonprofit organization

Profitability + Sustainability =
motivation for entities funding a for-profit organization.

Funding and Eligibility: Unveiling the Path Forward

To navigate the intricate world of funding, we must first develop a strong infrastructure that positions us for credibility and attractiveness to potential investors and funders. This chapter will provide you with a funding eligibility checklist and template designs, which serve as a practical guide. This isn't just about streamlining your flawless administration, as we discussed a few chapters back; it's about the steps needed to secure the financial backing your mission-rich entity deserves.

Funding can take various forms, from grants to contracts to business credit. Each avenue has its unique appeal and advantages. Some opt for grants because they appear easier; they don't need to be repaid. However, there are instances where you might prefer business credit, avoiding the necessity to intertwine your personal finances.

In my own journey with my LLC, I started with a small business loan that provided me with a financial cushion. This not only allowed me to take on contracts but also provided valuable technical assistance. It's crucial to approach funding with intention and purpose, leveraging the right financial tools to support your long-term goals. For example, using business credit can help you separate your business and personal finances, allowing for more strategic financial planning.

Positioning Yourself for Funding

To attract funding and resources effectively, you must follow a structured plan and checklist. It goes beyond business grants and contracts. We're talking about securing business credit, a line of credit, net-30 accounts, or business credit cards. These financial instruments offer the flexibility needed to sustain your operations. Just make sure that you are using the correct EIN information and that it is either an LLC or corporation. You cannot build business credit through a sole-proprietor business.

There are certain things that you can add to your portfolio for your business so that you are more marketable to funders and investors. These things will also have a level of attractiveness that will require them to actively seek you out. In essence, you want to position yourself in a way that allows you to leverage funding and resources effectively.

When it comes to funding, eligibility is the key. There are numerous funding opportunities out there, but if you're not eligible, they remain out of reach. To increase your eligibility, you can explore several strategies, including:

Business Certifications: You can opt for supplier diversity certifications, AAA certifications, and other business certifications. These certifications are especially valuable if your organization belongs to a minority, woman-owned, or veteran category. They open doors to government agencies and corporations required to allocate a percentage of contracts to certified organizations.

Local State Vendor Portals: Being part of these portals ensures you're in the loop when bids and grants become available. This puts you ahead of the competition as you're already vetted and part of the system.

SEO Certifications: Combining state vendor portal registration with SEO certifications increases your chances of accessing funding.

Fast Grant Programs: Many states offer fast grant programs that you can join, allowing you to access funds for your products or services. This extends your reach to potential customers who may not have the means to afford your services otherwise.

Alternative Financing: Forge relationships with banks or financiers who can provide quick credit approvals for your clients. This opens doors for customers who need your services but lack the initial capital.

By applying these strategies, you transform your organization into a magnet for funding and support. But there's no denying that the process of obtaining business certifications is challenging, depending on your location. However, the potential benefits far outweigh the effort.

Non-profits and Faith-Based Organizations: A Special Consideration

It's worth noting that churches and faith-based organizations are eligible for funding as well. However, funding for these entities often comes with restrictions, such as prohibitions on proselytizing. To navigate this, consider separating your church activities from state activities. Create a separate entity for community-based work to secure funding more effectively, often referred to as a parachurch.

Regardless of being a religious or community-based nonprofit, you can also opt for fiscal sponsorship from an established 501c3 organization as an initial or long-term approach to gaining experience in the world of funding. In essence, this means that you start a community-based nonprofit organization and would like to accept tax deductible donations for it. For a traditional nonprofit start-up, a fiscal sponsorship is a segue into a full non-profit organization before it obtains its own 501c3. For a non-profit *program or coalition* that doesn't intend to have its own 501c3 status, fiscal sponsorship serves as a long-term covering. Either way, the fiscal sponsoring agency will provide all of the administrative support for the non-profit entity, sometimes inclusive of insurances and other coverage.

As a point of caution, regardless of the intent for an organization to obtain a 501c3 status, the organization should establish a Memorandum of Agreement (MOA) or Memorandum of Understanding (MOU) with the fiscal sponsor. This agreement will require the fiscal sponsored entity to pay an administrative fee to the fiscal agent. This fee varies between 10-15% but can be higher when it comes to federal and state grants with a lot of reporting requirements. Tread lightly and do your research before signing an MOU or MOA with any organization. Do your research on the organization, reference checks (informal or formal), review public 990 information, and ask for their history as a fiscal sponsoring organization. Also take note that a fiscal sponsor and fiscal agent are not synonymous terms. *Money donated through a fiscal agent is NOT tax-deductible, but money donated through a fiscal sponsor is.*

Remember, a non-profit entity is not automatically designated 501c3 status under the tax code. They must apply for it. The non-profit is incorporated in its state and must follow guidelines within the state (which are not always readily accessible). The 501c3 status is a federal designation that must be obtained through the IRS.

I highly recommend that non-profit organizations start with a fiscal sponsor so that they are not overwhelmed with administrative oversight while identifying the organization's mission, purpose, and program implementation strategy. If you opt to start this way, still consider establishing a separate, fully independent entity from the fiscal sponsor. This means that you have your own EIN, bank account, and bylaws. Ensure the right individuals are on your board and are knowledgeable about non-profit regulations and financial responsibilities. Your nonprofit's compliance is critical to obtaining and maintaining its status.

State Tax Exemptions for Non-profits

For non-profits, it's crucial to obtain state tax exemptions. This can lead to significant savings on expenses such as hotel stays. By providing proof of non-profit status, you can benefit from discounted rates and memberships, saving valuable funds that can be channeled into your mission.

In the end, it's not just about acquiring funding; it's also about saving money and operating efficiently. These are the qualities that resonate with funders and investors, as they want to support organizations with sound financial practices and a clear vision.

Contracts and Certifications: A Gateway to Growth

Finally, after obtaining various certifications, you'll open the door to a new world of opportunities: contracts. These contracts can transform your mission-rich business. To get started, head to your state's website and explore the certification programs you qualify for. Sometimes there may be waiting periods, so it's crucial to act now and sign up for training programs that can kickstart your journey.

As you venture forth, remember that profit power isn't just about the bottom line; it's about having the resources and capabilities to drive your mission forward. It's about building a sustainable future for your organization and ensuring that your vision becomes a reality. And with the right funding, eligibility, and infrastructure in place, that future is well within your reach.

My journey was guided by intentionality when seeking that initial funding. I grew my network to include individuals who have expertise in business credit and financing. This became a game-changer for me and my clients. These types of connections allowed me to secure business credit for my enterprise, and I also extended this knowledge to my clients, introducing them to the world of business credit and not spending their personal funds on their businesses.

The value of this approach lies in the power of separation. We learned to differentiate between personal and business debt, recognizing that they carry distinct implications. For instance, having $20,000 in credit card debt for your business doesn't necessarily deter potential investors or lenders, if you have a well-thought-out plan for clearing that debt. However, the same cannot be said when applying for a personal loan or a mortgage. Lenders are more likely to hesitate if they see substantial business-related debt on your credit report. Your personal assets are also secured when the business owns the debt so that if a default occurred, the business would be bankrupt and not you or your family.

This is why it's crucial to move certain assets and financial responsibilities out of your personal name and into the incorporate name of your business (LLC or corporation). This shift helps you create a clear delineation between personal and business finances, ultimately making you more attractive to investors and lenders.

Remember, funding opportunities are abundant out there, but without the right eligibility and financial structure, they remain out of reach.

You must set yourself up for success by demonstrating your commitment to financial responsibility, which in turn will make you a magnet for those who want to support your mission.

Checklist for Compliance and Eligibility for Funding at Multiple Levels

Achieving compliance and eligibility for funding is crucial at various levels, be it private, local, state, or federal. Table 4 (below) and Table 5 on page 125 provide a comprehensive checklist for both for-profit and non-profit entities to ensure you meet the requirements at each level:

FUNDING ELIGIBILITY CHECKLIST

State

NON-PROFIT BUSINESS

- **State Nonprofit Status:** Register as a nonprofit organization within your state.
- **State-Level Filings:** File required reports, such as state charitable organization registrations or solicitation licenses.
- **State Grants and Funding:** Research and apply for state-level grants and funding opportunities.
- **Board Responsibilities:** Ensure your board of directors understands and complies with state-specific nonprofit regulations.

FOR-PROFIT BUSINESS

- **State Business Registration:** Register your business with the state and pay any applicable state taxes.
- **Industry-Specific Licenses:** Obtain licenses or permits relevant to your industry.
- **Sales Tax:** Comply with state sales tax regulations if applicable.
- **Workers' Compensation:** Ensure compliance with state workers' compensation requirements.
- **Annual Reporting:** Submit annual reports and updates as required by your state.

Federal

NON-PROFIT BUSINESS

- **501(c)(3) Status:** Maintain your 501(c)(3) status and file annual Form 990 returns.
- **Grant Compliance:** Adhere to grant compliance regulations if you receive federal grants.
- **Advocacy and Lobbying:** Understand the restrictions on political advocacy and lobbying for nonprofits.
- **Federal Funding:** Research federal grant opportunities, especially those aligned with your mission.

FOR-PROFIT BUSINESS

- **Federal Tax ID:** Obtain an Employer Identification Number (EIN) from the IRS.
- **Income Tax:** Pay federal income tax as required, adhering to IRS guidelines.
- **Industry Regulations:** Comply with federal regulations relevant to your industry.
- **UEI Number (formerly SAMs number)** – iA number issued by the System for Award Management (SAM) to identify businesses and other entities that do business with the federal government

Table 4

FUNDING ELIGIBILITY CHECKLIST

NON-PROFIT BUSINESS

- **501(c)(3) Status:** Obtain 501(c)(3) tax-exempt status from the IRS (or fiscal sponsor with one)
- **Bylaws and Governance:** Develop and adhere to nonprofit bylaws that outline your organization's structure and governance.
- **Board of Directors:** Compose a well-qualified board of directors who are knowledgeable about nonprofit regulations.
- **Financial Transparency:** Maintain transparency in your financial operations and be prepared to file annual Form 990s.
- **Mission Alignment:** Ensure that all activities align with your nonprofit's mission statement.

Private

FOR-PROFIT BUSINESS

- **Legal Structure:** Ensure your business is structured appropriately, such as an LLC, corporation, or sole proprietorship.
- **Financial Statements:** Maintain up-to-date and accurate financial records to demonstrate your business's financial health.
- **Tax Compliance:** Pay all taxes and keep clear tax records.
- **Business Credit:** Establish and maintain a strong business credit history.
- **Business Plan:** Create a robust business plan that outlines your goals, strategies, and financial projections.
- **Market Research:** Conduct thorough market research to understand your competition and target audience.

NON-PROFIT BUSINESS

- **Charitable Solicitation:** Register for charitable solicitation permits, if necessary, to legally raise funds within your state.
- **Local Reporting:** File annual reports with your state's charitable organizations division or attorney general's office.
- **Community Outreach:** Engage with local stakeholders and demonstrate your organization's impact on the community.

Local

FOR-PROFIT BUSINESS

- **Business License:** Obtain a local business license or permit, if required in your area.
- **Zoning Compliance:** Ensure your business location complies with local zoning regulations.
- **Regulatory Compliance:** Adhere to local business regulations and health and safety codes.
- **Community Engagement:** Establish a presence in your local community and contribute to its well-being.

Table 5

Primary Disqualifiers for Funding: Non-profit Entities

Non-profit organizations can encounter various disqualifiers that impede their ability to receive private, local, state, or federal funding. Here are some common factors that can disqualify nonprofits:

1. Lack of 501(c)(3) Status:	Most private, local, state, and federal funding sources require nonprofit organizations to have 501(c)(3) tax-exempt status from the IRS. Without this status, nonprofits may not be eligible for tax-deductible donations or certain grants.
2. Non-Compliance:	Failure to comply with state and federal nonprofit regulations, including annual reporting and financial transparency requirements, can disqualify a nonprofit from receiving funding.
3. Conflicts of Interest:	If a non-profit's leadership or board members have conflicts of interest that compromise the organization's integrity or mission, it may be disqualified from funding opportunities.
4. Political Activity:	Engaging in partisan political activities or excessive lobbying can jeopardize a nonprofit's 501(c)(3) status and its eligibility for certain grants.
5. Misuse of Funds:	Mishandling or misusing funds, such as diverting donations for personal use or unrelated expenses, can disqualify a nonprofit from funding.
6. Discrimination:	Discriminatory practices or policies that violate anti-discrimination laws can disqualify non-profits from funding, particularly government grants.

7. Failure to Meet Grant Requirements:	Non-profits may be disqualified if they fail to meet the specific requirements and objectives outlined in grant applications.
8. Loss of Public Trust:	Scandals, mismanagement, or unethical behavior that erode public trust can deter donors and disqualify non-profits from funding.

Primary Disqualifiers for Funding: For-Profit Entities

For-profit businesses also have specific disqualifiers that can hinder their access to funding from various sources:

Legal Non-Compliance:	Failure to comply with local, state, and federal laws and regulations, such as business registration and taxation, can disqualify for-profit entities from funding.
Insufficient Creditworthiness:	Poor personal or business credit history can make it challenging to secure business loans, credit, and investment capital.
Business Structure:	Some funding sources may have specific eligibility criteria based on the legal structure of the business, such as sole proprietorships or certain types of corporations.
Environmental or Ethical Concerns:	For-profit businesses that engage in activities with negative environmental or ethical implications may be disqualified from certain grants or investment opportunities.

Competitive Factors:	In a highly competitive market or industry, businesses that lack a unique selling proposition or struggle to differentiate themselves may find it difficult to secure funding.
Unsustainable Business Model:	If a for-profit entity lacks a viable business model or demonstrates consistent losses, it may be disqualified from funding due to concerns about profitability.
Inadequate Planning:	Incomplete or poorly structured business plans and strategies can make it challenging to secure funding, as investors and lenders look for well-thought-out proposals.
Criminal Activity:	Involvement in criminal activities or a history of legal issues can disqualify for-profit entities from funding, particularly from government grants and contracts.
Non-Alignment with Funding Goals:	Businesses that do not align with the goals and objectives of specific funding programs may not be eligible for support.

It's crucial for both non-profit and for-profit entities to thoroughly research the eligibility criteria and disqualifiers for the funding sources they are targeting. Maintaining compliance, ethical conduct, and a strong alignment with the funder's objectives are essential to increasing the chances of securing funding.

Obtaining technical assistance at the local, state, and federal levels is crucial for organizations seeking to access funding. Here are primary resources and avenues to consider.

Local Level:	1. Local Small Business Development Centers (SBDCs): SBDCs provide free or low-cost consulting and training services to small businesses, including nonprofits. They offer guidance on business planning, financial management, and accessing funding opportunities.
	2. Chamber of Commerce: Local chambers often offer resources and networking opportunities for businesses and nonprofits. They can provide guidance on local funding options and opportunities.
	3. Municipal or County Economic Development Offices: These offices can connect you with resources, grants, and incentives available at the local level. They may also offer assistance in navigating local regulations and permits.
	4. Community Organizations: Local community organizations and foundations often provide grants and technical assistance to nonprofits in their area. They can help identify funding sources and provide guidance on the application process.
State Level:	1. State Small Business Development Centers (SBDCs): State-level SBDCs offer services similar to their local counterparts but on a larger scale. They can connect you with statewide resources and funding opportunities.
	2. State Economic Development Agencies: State economic development agencies can provide information on grants, tax incentives, and funding programs available to businesses and nonprofits within the state.
	3. State Nonprofit Associations: Many states have nonprofit associations that offer resources, training, and assistance specifically tailored to nonprofit organizations. They often maintain databases of grant opportunities.
	4. State Grant Programs: Research state-level grant programs that align with your organization's mission. State agencies and departments may offer grants in various sectors, from education to healthcare.

Federal Level:	1. U.S. Small Business Administration (SBA): The SBA provides resources and assistance to small businesses, including guidance on securing loans, grants, and contracts. The SBA's website offers valuable information and tools.
	2. Grants.gov: This federal website is a central portal for finding and applying for federal grants. It lists a wide range of grant opportunities from various federal agencies.
	3. Federal Funding Agencies: Identify federal agencies relevant to your organization's mission. Many federal agencies offer grant programs, technical assistance, and support. Examples include the National Institutes of Health (NIH), the National Endowment for the Arts (NEA), and the Department of Education.
	4. Congressional Offices: Reach out to your U.S. Senators and Representatives' offices. They often have staff dedicated to assisting constituents in accessing federal resources and funding.
	5. Federal Procurement Technical Assistance Centers (PTACs): PTACs offer technical assistance to businesses seeking federal contracts. They can help with registration, bidding, and compliance.
	6. Foundation Center: While not a government agency, the Foundation Center (now Candid) provides extensive resources and training on nonprofit fundraising, including grant-seeking strategies and funding opportunities.
	7. Local Federal Assistance Programs: Some local government offices or community organizations receive federal funds and can guide you in accessing federal resources specific to your region.

Remember to leverage these resources in your quest for funding. Networking with local and state officials, chambers of commerce, and non-profit associations can often lead to valuable insights and connections. Additionally, conducting thorough research and staying updated on funding opportunities at all levels is essential to a successful grant-seeking strategy.

Benefits of Entrepreneurial Tax Strategies

Exploring entrepreneurial tax strategies has been a game-changer for my mission-driven business. It's not just about securing grants and contracts; it's about understanding the financial benefits that can be just as impactful. These strategies offer a myriad of advantages, aligning perfectly with our mission and goals.

First and foremost, they lead to significant cost savings. By minimizing our tax burden, we can channel those saved funds directly into our critical programs and initiatives, ensuring we can continue making a positive impact. It's about leveraging resources, diversifying our income sources, and fortifying our financial sustainability for the long haul. We're better positioned for lasting success, and it's a reassuring feeling.

But it's not just about money; it's also about operational efficiency. By optimizing our tax strategy, we can allocate our resources more effectively, keeping us laser-focused on our mission and what truly matters. These tax savings are like a lifeline, keeping us resilient and prepared for the unexpected.

Moreover, entrepreneurial tax strategies give us a competitive edge. We become more attractive to funders and investors who see our financial acumen and the potential for long-term growth. But this is not a one-size-fits-all endeavor. It's about tailoring our approach to our unique needs and finding the business structure that fits like a glove and aligns perfectly with our funding goals.

For for-profit entities, there are even more benefits to uncover. Take, for instance, the home office deduction under Tax Publication 587. It's a clever way to save money on everyday expenses like utilities and vehicle miles. The tax landscape is brimming with opportunities, like Tax Publication 15, which lets us pay our children as employees, allowing them to enjoy the perks while we reap the deductions. It's a win-win, and it's part of our strategy.

Then there's Tax Publication 535, showing us how every trip can become a business trip. By turning personal journeys into deductions, we're maximizing our resources, and every dollar saved is another dollar that can be reinvested in our mission.

For non-profit organizations, understanding the rules is crucial. Did you know that nonprofits don't have to pay taxes in their state? It's one of the many intricacies of nonprofit life that can lead to substantial savings. Enrolling in business programs with the companies we already purchase products from can also be a game-changer, ensuring we're not overpaying taxes. The world of nonprofit rates and discounts opens new avenues for us, making it easier to access the tools we need.

However, it's not just about the benefits; it's about understanding and staying in good standing with our state. Operating within the state where we intend to do business is a fundamental rule. Attempting to establish a business in another state can lead to complications, costly procedures, and a "foreign LLC transfer." This complex process often requires legal expertise and can result in dual tax obligations in both the home state and the state of business origination, something we've learned to navigate with care.

In the end, entrepreneurial tax strategies aren't just about dollars and cents; they're about securing our mission's future. By staying active, remaining focused, and making the most of available resources, we ensure our organization stays resilient and never goes dormant. This journey has been about more than finances; it's been about securing the impact we want to make.

Navigating the World of Certifications

When you become an approved entity with your local state vendor agency or acquire 8(a) and SDO certifications, funders are more likely to contact you about funding for several compelling reasons. This enables you to participate in programs like the SBPP (Small Business Purchasing Program):

1. Credibility: Being an approved entity or holding certifications demonstrates that your organization has undergone a rigorous vetting process. This, in turn, signifies credibility and reliability, which are crucial factors for funders looking to invest their resources.

2. Eligibility: Approvals and certifications often come with specific eligibility criteria, and by meeting these criteria, you showcase that your organization aligns with the objectives and priorities funders are seeking.

3. Market Demand: Many government agencies and large corporations have mandates or quotas for working with approved or certified entities. This means there's a built-in demand for your products or services, making you an attractive partner for funders who want to support organizations aligned with these mandates.

4. Reduced Risk: Funders prefer to invest in organizations with a proven track record of compliance and effective operation. Approved entities and certified businesses have demonstrated their ability to adhere to regulations and deliver quality outcomes, which reduces the risk for funders.

5. Diverse Opportunities: Depending on the type of approval or certification, you may gain access to exclusive opportunities and contracts that are reserved for entities like yours. Funders are aware of this and may see value in supporting your organization's growth to tap into these opportunities.

As for the simplified process of obtaining 8(a) and SDO certifications:

8(a) Certification:

The 8(a) Business Development program is administered by the Small Business Administration (SBA) and is designed to assist small businesses in securing government contracts. The process involves several steps:

1. Eligibility Check	Ensure your business meets the SBA's criteria, which generally include being a small business, being at least 51% owned and controlled by a socially and economically disadvantaged individual, and demonstrating good character.

2. Preparation:	Gather the necessary documentation, such as financial statements, tax returns, business licenses, and a detailed business plan.
3. Online Application:	Complete the online application through the SBA's Certify site. This will require providing detailed information about your business and its owners.
4. Submission:	Submit your application and pay the associated fee.
5. Review:	The SBA will review your application and may request additional information.
6. Decision:	Once your application is approved, you will be granted 8(a) certification, which is typically valid for nine years.

SDO (Supplier Diversity Office) Certifications:

SDO certifications can occur in two ways, through self-certification or the state:

1. **State (or Locality for large cities) Certification: These are the steps for** getting certified as a minority or women-owned business through the supplier diversity office.

    1. Register for pre-certification training class.
    2. Attend class.
    3. Use the attendance code to complete SDO application.
    4. Go through a review process with SDO staff.
    5. Edit per requests of the SDO agent.
    6. Get your approval!

*Note that you may be able to represent more than one company during the training. Also, depending on which state your business operates in, you may be able to get automatic approval in another state by applying there.

2. **Self-Certification:** There are some organizations that will allow entities to self-certify as a Small Disadvantaged Business (SDB). Those businesses would follow these simplified steps:

> 1. Eligibility Check: Ensure your business qualifies as a small, disadvantaged business. This means that you must be at least 51% owned and controlled by one or more socially and economically disadvantaged individuals.
>
> 2. Registration: Register your business in the System for Award Management (SAM) database.
>
> 3. Self-Certification: While registering in SAM, you will have the option to self-certify as an SDB. This involves providing the required information and certifications as part of your SAM registration.
>
> 4. Document Your Disadvantaged Status: Be prepared to provide documentation and evidence of your disadvantaged status upon request by contracting officers or potential clients.

It's important to note that while these steps provide a simplified overview, the actual process may require detailed documentation and can vary depending on your specific circumstances. Consulting with the SBA or a Small Business Development Center (SBDC) can be highly beneficial during the certification process.

It's important to note that annual filing requirements are a crucial aspect of maintaining eligibility for funding and contracts, especially for organizations seeking to secure grants, contracts, or financial support. These requirements vary depending on the type of entity and certification, and compliance is essential to demonstrate accountability and operational transparency.

For example, businesses, including those with SDO (Self-Certification) or 8(a) certifications, may need to submit annual filings or reports that outline their financial status, activities, and compliance with relevant regulations. Failing to meet these requirements can jeopardize your eligibility for certain funding opportunities.

However, it's worth mentioning that sole proprietors, while eligible for many opportunities, may face challenges when accessing funding. Since sole proprietorships are often small businesses with a single owner, they might have limited capacity and resources, which can affect their ability to meet certain eligibility criteria or compete for larger contracts.

To overcome these challenges, sole proprietors can consider the following strategies:

Challenges for Sole-proprietor Business Operators	
Formalize the Business:	Structuring the business as a legal entity, such as an LLC (Limited Liability Company) or corporation, can enhance credibility and access to certain funding opportunities.
Leverage Certifications:	Explore certifications, such as Small Business Administration (SBA) certifications, which can provide access to specific contracts and funding programs.
Seek Collaboration:	Collaborating with other businesses or forming partnerships can enhance your capacity to take on larger projects or access funding opportunities that may be out of reach as a sole proprietor.
Continuous Learning:	Stay informed about available resources, including grants, loans, and training programs, which can help sole proprietors improve their business operations and financial management.
Utilize Online Resources:	Access online platforms and databases that list various funding opportunities and grants that are open to sole proprietors. Websites like Grants.gov and SBA.gov can be valuable resources.

Annual filing requirements and challenges for sole proprietors underscore the importance of proactive financial management and continuous improvement. By maintaining proper records, exploring relevant certifications, and staying informed about available resources, sole proprietors can increase their eligibility for funding and contracts, ultimately expanding their opportunities for growth and success.

Where to Find Information:

I understand that navigating the world of certifications and approvals can be daunting, especially when you're eager to secure funding and opportunities for your mission-rich business. It's a journey that requires determination and attention to detail, but the rewards are worth the effort. As you embark on this path, consider visiting the following websites for guidance and support:

For 8(a) Certification:

- Small Business Administration (SBA) (https://www.sba.gov/): The SBA's official website provides comprehensive information on the 8(a) program, eligibility requirements, and step-by-step guidance for the application process.

- SCORE (https://www.score.org/): SCORE is a nonprofit organization partnered with the SBA. They offer free mentorship and resources for small businesses, including those seeking 8(a) certification.

For SDO (Self-Certification):

- System for Award Management (SAM) (https://www.sam.gov/: SAM is where you'll register your business, including your self-certification as a Small Disadvantaged Business (SDB). The SAM website provides detailed instructions on the registration process.

- Small Business Development Center (SBDC) (https://www.sba. gov/local-assistance/find/): The SBDC network, in partnership with the SBA, offers free consulting and training services to help small businesses, including those looking to self-certify as SDBs.

Remember, you're not alone on this journey. There are resources and experts available to guide you through the process and help you achieve your certification goals. Your dedication to making a positive impact through your mission-rich business is inspiring, and I wish you the very best in your endeavors.

SCAMS to Watch Out for:

While seeking to set up your business and obtain certifications, beware of scams. Any business structure tasks taken are a crucial step for many businesses. It's essential to be aware of potential scams and fraudulent practices. Some common scams and red flags to watch out for include:

Fee-Based Certification Services:	Be cautious of organizations or consultants that charge high fees to assist with the certification process. In most cases, you can complete the application process on your own without the need for expensive services.
Promises of Guaranteed Approval:	No one can guarantee that your certification application will be approved. Beware of individuals or companies that claim a guaranteed certification in exchange for payment.

Unsolicited Offers:	If you receive unsolicited emails or phone calls offering assistance with certifications, especially from unfamiliar sources, be skeptical. Legitimate organizations typically don't reach out in this manner.
Inaccurate Information:	Scammers may provide inaccurate or outdated information about the certification process, requirements, or eligibility criteria.
Fake Certificates:	Some scammers may produce counterfeit certificates or documents to make it seem like you've been certified. Always verify the legitimacy of any certification you receive.
Pressure to Act Quickly:	Scammers often create a sense of urgency, pressuring you to make quick decisions or payments. Legitimate certification processes have specific timelines and requirements.
Request for Sensitive Information:	Be cautious about sharing sensitive information, such as Social Security numbers or financial details, with unverified individuals or organizations.

To protect yourself from potential scams when pursuing SDO and 8(a) certifications or any type of business structure set-up:

- Research and verify the legitimacy of any organization or con- sultant offering assistance. Check their credentials and reviews from other businesses.

- Consult with official government websites and resources, such as the Small Business Administration (SBA) or System for Award Management (SAM), to understand the certification process and requirements.

- Avoid making payments or sharing sensitive information unless you're certain of the entity's authenticity.

- Reach out to your local Small Business Development Center (SBDC) or the SBA for guidance and resources. They can provide free assistance and ensure you follow the correct process.

- If you suspect fraudulent activity, report it to the appropriate authorities, such as the Federal Trade Commission (FTC) or your state attorney general's office.

Remember that obtaining certifications is a legitimate and valuable process that can open doors to funding and contracts for your business. Stay vigilant, do your research, and rely on reputable sources to help you achieve your certification goals.

Call to Action:

Visit monroenaylor.com for worksheets related to funding, writing grants, and funding plans.

Epilogue

This book is a valuable tool for establishing a mission-rich and profit-powered venture. Throughout its pages, you have acquired the knowledge to transform your passion into a sustainable, faith-based, community-focused non-profit or LLC business. Don't settle for being a glorified volunteer of your business, working extended hours without compensation.

Here's a concise summary of the key insights from the book that will empower you to launch and manage a fully-funded mission-rich entity:

Chapter 1: Mindset

This chapter reinforces the mindset of mission-rich individuals and explores the various entity types commonly initiated by individuals. It dispels myths surrounding mission-rich ventures and introduces you to the ABCDs, providing guidance on elevating your mindset for a resilient journey to profitability.

Chapter 2: Complexes and Sabotage

This chapter focuses on identifying and overcoming the most prevalent complexes that sabotage one's ability to establish a mission-focused business structure and secure operational funds. Recognizing these complexes can break the cycle of procrastination, hindering your entity's profitability.

Chapter 3: Breaking Free of the Comfort Zone

Digging into the fears, biases, and familiarities that lead to stagnation in mindset and business revenue, this chapter emphasizes the importance of stepping beyond your comfort zone. Confronting your limits and moving beyond your familiarity is crucial for business growth and development.

Chapter 4: Lead with Authenticity and Empathy

This chapter underscored the significance of authenticity and empathy for mission-focused individuals. While conventional wisdom might advocate cut-throat approaches, this chapter argued that authenticity and empathy contribute to longevity, effectiveness, and business attractiveness.

Chapter 5: Strong Networks

With highlights on the value of relationships, this chapter emphasized the need for trusted individuals in both professional and personal circles. Building strong networks is essential for efficiency and achieving your business goals.

Chapter 6: Work & Life Balance

With a focus on the importance of work-life balance, this chapter emphasizes that running a successful business should not entail overworking yourself to exhaustion. Building a business should allow you to enjoy the things and people most valuable to you.

Chapter 7: Flawless Administration

While addressing a frequently overlooked aspect of business, this chapter focused on administration. It stressed why proper budgeting and infrastructure are critical for profitability and provided guidance on effective administration.

Chapter 8: Planning & Strategy

In identifying another overlooked aspect of business, this chapter emphasizes the importance of focusing on funding and grant strategies for long-term financial success. Mission-focused individuals are encouraged to balance working in and on their businesses.

Chapter 9: Dollars Can Follow You

This concluding chapter guided you on how to position your business to attract funding. It outlined strategies to access funding sources that can be challenging for mission-focused entities to tap into.

Allow this book to serve as a roadmap for your journey toward building a mission-rich, financially successful enterprise.

About the Author

LaTonia Monroe Naylor's journey is one that embodies resilience, dedication, and an unwavering commitment to making the world a better place. Born in Springfield, MA, her path has been anything but conventional, taking her across the globe as the daughter of a military man. This diverse upbringing has instilled in her a deep appreciation for different cultures and perspectives, which has profoundly influenced her life's work.

LaTonia's educational journey mirrors her remarkable life story. Her determination led her to graduate from Springfield Central High School, and her thirst for knowledge propelled her to earn a Bachelor of Arts in Business Administration from Our Lady of the Elms College in 2003. Her academic pursuits did not stop there; she later achieved a Master of Science in Nonprofit Management and Philanthropy, accompanied by a Certificate of Board Governance and Volunteerism from Bay Path College in 2012. In 2014, she successfully completed the prestigious Springfield Leadership Institute program, and her commitment to personal and professional growth led her to become a proud graduate of the Leadership Pioneer Valley's class of 2016.

In her role as a Chief Business Educator, LaTonia is not only committed to serving her community but also possesses a unique ability to impart her extensive knowledge and wisdom to others. Her passion for helping others stems from a personal tragedy she endured at the age of 16. This life-altering event ignited a fire within her to make a positive impact on the world. She started her career in the for-profit sector but soon found her true calling in the public sector, where her unwavering dedication to uplifting people led her to co-found two nonprofit organizations: Parent Villages Inc. in 2018 and VITAL Center, Inc. in 2006. Her influence extends far and wide as she advises numerous nonprofit start-ups, sole-proprietorships, and small businesses.

Throughout her journey, LaTonia has secured and managed multi-million-dollar grants and programs, empowering others to achieve their missions. Her impressive skill set includes being a certified facilitator, an experienced trainer, certified grant writer, a dynamic public speaker, and a certified tax professional. She also served as an adjunct professor, sharing her knowledge and inspiring future leaders.

In March 2022, LaTonia founded Monroe Naylor Consulting LLC., driven by her passion to offer her expertise to a broader audience. Her commitment to empowering individuals to launch and lead mission-rich nonprofits and small businesses coupled with her dedication to navigating the complexities of entrepreneurial and nonprofit tax compliance date back to approximately 2008.

Even with her extensive professional commitments, LaTonia remains deeply connected to her community. She donates her time as a mentor to youth and young adults, actively contributes to her church, and has spearheaded initiatives like computer learning centers and youth summer programs. Her heart is firmly anchored in her community, and her love for Springfield shines through in her tireless efforts to bring about positive change.

LaTonia's remarkable journey transcends her professional achievements, as she is not only a dedicated professional but also a devoted wife and mother, guided by the enduring inspiration of her Nana, Joyce Marie Vaughn. Her life is intertwined with that of her loving husband, Reverend Mah'dee Naylor, Sr., and their four beautiful children (Naomi, Patience, Mah'dee Jr., and Melodie) and fur baby (Nala). LaTonia's unwavering commitment to her family serves as a wellspring of motivation, propelling her tireless work in education and community service. In 2017, she began advocating as an at-large member of the Springfield School Committee, now in her second term. Her dedication has also led her to focus on two-generational programs, recognizing their significance in creating lasting impact and sustainability for families.

In honoring the legacy of her beloved Nana, LaTonia exemplifies values of dedication, compassion, and resilience, serving as an inspiring force for positive change within Springfield and beyond.

LaTonia's impact extends beyond her immediate community. She has been recognized and appointed to leadership positions at the state level She serves on the boards of organizations and coalitions where she is an influential figure on policy and resources centered on leadership, education, youth and family empowerment, and economic self-sufficiency.

While LaTonia's tireless efforts are driven by her commitment to her community, she is no stranger to recognition. Her humility is evident in her accolades from numerous organizations, including being a member of the BusinessWest 40 Under 40 Class of 2016, the Class of 2020 Massachusetts Commonwealth Unsung Heroine, and a 2021 Commonwealth Black Excellence Awardee, 2021 Massachusetts All-State School Committee, and a 2022 Urban League of Springfield Community

Book LaTonia to:

- Speak at your next event

- Present at your next conference

- Facilitate your next training

- Coaching services

To work with LaTonia, visit www.monroenaylor.com to complete our questionnaire and be invited to a 15-minute interest interview.

Follow Monroe Naylor Consulting LLC on social media to stay up-to-date on webinars, master classes, and free content.

To access your free resources and digital toolkits visit: www.missionrichandprofitpowered.com

www.monroenaylor.com/resources

Bibliography:

Aswell, S. (2020, October 10). *Grant Statistics: What the Numbers Reveal.* Submittable Blog. Retrieved October 1, 2023, from https://blog.submittable.com/grant-statistics/

Brinckerhoff, P. (2009). *Mission-Based Management: Leading Your Not-for-Profit, 3rd Edition*: John Wiley & Sons, Inc.

Bryant, S. (2022, November 26). *How Many Startups Fail and Why?* Reviewed by David Kindness and fact-checked by Melody Kazel. Investopedia. Retrieved October 1, 2023, from https://www.investopedia.com/articles/personal-finance/040915/how-many-startups-fail-and-why.asp#:~:text=According%20to%20business%20owners%2C%20reasons,an%20expert%20in%20the%20industry.

Burg, B., & Mann, J. D. (2015). *The Go-Giver, Expanded Edition: A Little Story About a Powerful Business Idea* (Go-Giver, Book 1). New York: Portfolio.

Carr, J. (2018, February 23. *"Everything attached to me wins".* One Nature Under God: You Will Win, (YouTube)

Collins, J. (2001). *Good to Great.* London, England: Random House Business Books.

Council of Nonprofits. (n.d.). *Myths about Nonprofits.* Retrieved October 1, 2023, from https://www.councilofnonprofits.org/about-americas-nonprofits/myths-about-nonprofits

Covey, S. R. (1997). *The 7 Habits of Highly Effective Families: Building a Beautiful Family Culture in a Turbulent World.* New York: Golden Books.

Goleman, D., & Boyatzis, R. E. (2017, February 6). *Emotional Intelligence Has 12 Elements. Which Do You Need to Work On?* Harvard Business Review. Retrieved October 1, 2023, from https://hbr.org/2017/02/emotional-intelligence-has-12-elements-which-do-you-need-to-work-on

Hogan, R. (1969). *Development of An Empathy Scale.* Journal of Consulting and Clinical Psychology, 33, 307–316.

Kiyosaki, Robert T. *Rich Dad, Poor Dad.* Plata Publishing, 2017.

La Piana, D. (2008). T*he Nonprofit Strategy Revolution: Real-Time Strategic Planning in a Rapid-Response World.* Paperback edition. Published on March 15, 2008.

Tracy, B. (2006). *The Psychology of Selling: Increase Your Sales Faster and Easier Than You Ever Thought Possible.* Paperback edition. Published on July 16, 2006.

www.ingramcontent.com/pod-product-compliance
Lightning Source LLC
Chambersburg PA
CBHW072149090426
42740CB00012B/2202